The Unbound Soul

Richard L. Haight

ISBN 978-0999210000
2nd Edition

Disclaimer:

1. Some names and identifying details have been changed to protect the privacy of individuals.

2. This book is not intended as a substitute for the medical or psychological advice of physicians/psychiatrists. The reader should regularly consult their healthcare provider in matters relating to physical or mental health and particularly with respect to any symptoms that may require diagnosis or medical attention.

Published by Shinkaikan Body, Mind, Spirit LLC
www.richardhaight.net

Contents

Shinkaido by Shizen Osaki (penned July 2012)

The tao that can be told is not the eternal Tao.
The name that can be named is not the eternal Name.

The unnamable is the eternally real.
Naming is the origin of all particular things.

Free from desire, you realize the mystery.
Caught in desire, you see only the manifestations.

Yet mystery and manifestations arise from the same source.
This source is called darkness.

Darkness within darkness.
The gateway to all understanding.

— *Tao Te Ching*

Introduction

We are on the brink of a great revelation;
I am not the revealer.
We are on the brink of a great revelation;
this is my role.
We are on the brink of a great revelation;
What is your role?

If you were drawn to read this book, you are probably not at all surprised by the assertion that we are on the brink of a great revelation. In fact, many who are reading this book have been anticipating this revelation for most of their lives. Bear in mind that with any revelation, there also comes the breaking down of interfering structures of mind. All of us have these structures, and we have come to depend upon them, even if we haven't realized it.

There are several distinct writing styles applied in this book expressly for resolving the blocking structures of our lives. Sometimes the teachings come in through inspiration meant to elevate the reader into the frequencies of consciousness; conversely, I introduce the reader to certain vital tools that, when practiced regularly, greatly assist in the unfoldment process; and finally there are the teachings that elucidate the disharmonious nature of the mind so that we can begin to see it through observation. When we understand more fully how the mind blocks us from realization of the fundamental truth throughout all that is, it is much easier to tune to the alternative, which is consciousness. The teachings of the mind are quite elaborate, and, unless we are totally familiar with the nature of the mind, we will be unaware as to when we are tuned to the mind. In such a case we will continue to be entrapped in mind, not realizing that there is another option, consciousness. One of the primary purposes of this book is to so elucidate the differences between consciousness and mind that the reader will immediately begin noticing when they are tuned to mind, which is the source of suffering, and in so realizing, choose to tune to consciousness instead. As we continually observe the mind and choose to tune in to consciousness, liberation reveals itself.

In this work I often use the word "spiritual" for ease of communication. It is an easily misconstrued word. In truth all things are equally spiritual, so we should be careful not to attach a feeling of special to it. "Unfoldment" and "realization" are two other words that are commonly employed as well. "Unfoldment", as I use it, indicates the removal of barriers to reveal that which has been obscured, while "realization" indicates being aware of something that had previously gone unnoticed. None of these words are associated with becoming, growing, or attaining.

In this work, I include many of the visions that have served in my unfoldment process. I have endeavored to record them as accurately as possible, free of personal belief. The value of these visions is in their service to your unfoldment process.

This book is written entirely through connection with the unnamable, the Tao. Of course, for the sake of communication, we must have a word, so Lao-Tzu used Tao, and I use Soul or Isness. But let's not get caught up in these names, as they mean nothing in particular. This book was written for those who are ready for revelation. As this book has been written for the purpose of revealing what lies beneath, it will bring up hidden disharmonies within the reader. We may feel anxiety and fear. We may feel frustration or anger. We may feel as if something is blocking us from going further. That something is what lurks beneath, not wanting to be seen. These blockages are the internal structures that apocalypse breaks down to reveal the truth within.

I recommend that readers, before reading, put themselves into as calm and unconditionally loving a space as possible. And only after the dust settles do we read. When the dust rises, we calm again, allowing the dust to settle before we continue. In this way, we can read and receive the true power of this message, a power that goes well beyond words.

Richard L. Haight (November 17, 2015)

~Part 1~
My Story

Since my late teens, I have been compelled to write down all the spiritual visions and insights that I have had in my life. I knew it would result in a book that would help to elevate mankind out of the frequencies of disharmony and into the frequencies of harmony. What I didn't understand at the time was how my personal story would be of service to anyone else and how those stories would tie together in a meaningful way that would assist people in their unfoldment process. I did not want a bunch of interesting personal stories that were of no practical service to anyone else. What would be the point of that?

Not until I began teaching weekend intensive meditation retreats did all of the missing information that ties everything together in a harmonious whole, in a deeply practical message to the world, begin to flow. I was to write the story of my life and tell how that story wove the tapestry of spiritual unfoldment and how spiritual unfoldment wove the tapestry of my life. One cannot be extricated from the other, because it's through our lives that spiritual unfoldment occurs.

My deepest prayer is that this story be of assistance to others, helping them to understand how spiritual unfoldment and vision flow through their lives. My life is no more special than anyone else's, but it serves as a workable example of practical daily unfoldment. It's my prayer that your life is an even better example.

~Chapter 1~
The Promise

I grew up on a horse ranch in rural Southern California, where sagebrush and chaparral foothills seemed to stretch on forever. During summer months, the neighborhood kids would spend dawn to dusk in those hills, playing cowboys and Indians, hide-and-seek, and war; building forts; constructing teepees from dill weed and dried grass; hiking the eucalyptus-strewn hills and valleys; and swimming in the lakes. Life was simple and full of adventure, until one day when everything changed.

After our wargame ended one afternoon, an older kid told us that his mother would be teaching Bible study at their house the following evening and that we should all attend. I had no idea what the Bible was, but after being told that we'd burn in Hell for not attending, we all signed up on the spot.

Mrs. Pacetti lived in a beautiful, Spanish-style stucco compound at the top of a hill surrounded by four acres of avocado groves. A large stucco garage stood sentry between the narrow driveway and the house, blocking visibility. Mrs. Pacetti kept the palatial house immaculately clean, to the point where it made me nervous being there for fear of accidentally touching something.

She taught the older children while her daughter taught the younger ones like me. I was only about eight years old, and I couldn't understand much other than Jesus was the heroic Son of God, who used the power of love to save people and perform great miracles. Each of us was given a Bible that we could read as homework. I had a learning disorder, and reading was very difficult for me, but I made time every night before sleep to try to read the Bible. I liked reading the Bible, despite my disdain for reading in school.

All went well until, one night, some months into the classes, when Mrs. Pacetti had us all meet in the main room of the house for a combined study session. She explained that we, as shepherds of the Lord, had a duty to find the lost sheep and lead them to salvation. We were to convert our parents, for if they weren't Born Again then surely they would burn in Hell for eternity. Some of the parents were already Christians of other denominations, but according to Mrs. Pacetti that did not matter, as only Born Again Christians were truly saved; I was terrified. I didn't want them to go to Hell. But how was I, an eight-year-old boy, going to convince my parents to convert?

I went home that night, determined. I had no idea how I was going to convince my parents, but they were going to convert. After dinner, I asked if I could speak to them about religion. They were surprised but said religion was an adult subject, and that we would have to discuss it as adults. They asked me if I were willing to have this adult discussion. Pride welled up within as I said, "Yes." My father asked me if I had a Bible, which I quickly retrieved from my bedroom while he got his two Bibles. Together we had three different Bible translations.

I told them that Mrs. Pacetti had warned us that our parents would go to Hell if they didn't become Born Again Christians. Gently, my father asked if I believed God to be a loving Being.

"Yes," I said.

He then asked, "Is it loving to send someone to Hell for eternity just because the person wasn't a Born Again Christian?" I was losing confidence, and tears began to well up. He then asked, "If you were God, would you send us to Hell for not being Born Again Christians?"

I said, "Of course not."

He went on: "Would you love or respect a God that would send people to Hell just for being of a different religion?" After thinking about it, I realized I would not respect that God. In fact, I wouldn't even like that God. He told me of the many people in far-off lands who might never even hear of Christianity. He asked if people should be punished if they had no knowledge of Christianity and, therefore, no ability to choose to become Born Again. He then told me about Islam, a religion that teaches that all who worship deities other than the one true God, Allah, go to Hell. Who is right? Who is wrong? Is everyone going to Hell?

We opened our Bibles and began comparing verses. He had me read the text and then compare it to his Bible's translation. They were slightly different, and from this difference, different understandings could be reached. Looking at the resurrection story of Matthew as compared to resurrection stories of Mark, Luke, or John, we could see the accounts were drastically different. After Jesus is removed from the cross, his body is entombed, and the entrance covered over with a large boulder. Because Jesus claimed that he would resurrect in three days, some of his followers went to the tomb to investigate and ritualistically care for the body, if it were there. The stories of each book differ quite dramatically as to what occurred at the tomb. In Matthew there is an earthquake, and an angel descends to roll away the stone and sit on it. In Mark, the stone is already moved away, and there is a young man dressed in white with no other indication as to who he is. In Luke, the stone had been rolled away, and inside there are two men in dazzling attire. In John, the stone was moved away from the entrance, and no one went inside to check on Jesus' body. Which story was correct? I had no idea.

At the end of our conversation, he confided that he didn't presume to know the truth and didn't think anyone else knew, either. He asked me if I really wanted to know the truth about God. I nodded. He said, "Then you must be very honest, keep an open mind, and keep searching."

Later that year I began to have a series of very powerful dreams, wherein I would wake up in a dream state that had far more depth than waking reality to find a man lying on the floor in the middle of my bedroom. The room was filled with a loving warmth, and I felt a strong desire to approach him. When I came close enough to look into his eyes, I could sense compassion and infinite understanding, and instinctively I knew he was Jesus Christ.

His eyes glowed with love, and yet there was also a deep sorrow. I looked at his body and realized something was wrong — it was sagging. I returned my gaze to his eyes, and he pleaded, "Help me." I tried to help him up, but his forearm squished in my hands like a water-balloon. I realized he had no skeleton. Try as I might, I couldn't budge him. I awoke hearing, "Help me," yet feeling utterly helpless.

How could a child help Jesus Christ, I wondered. This dream repeated many times over a period of months, and each time it ended with the feeling of profound helplessness. The memory seared my soul and replayed itself during my waking hours. I pulled into myself, fearing that no one would understand what I was feeling, or that I would be ridiculed and shunned. I was alone.

In school I would daydream in class, wondering what Jesus wanted, but no answer came. Finally, one night in a dream, I got my answer. The dream was the same — except for the last moment, in which previously I always awoke. This time an intense energy surged through, anchoring me in the dream. "How can I help you?" I asked.

"Find my bones, for they are the core of my teaching. Most of what is written about me is untrue. Mankind has so twisted my teachings for selfish gain that little of the essence remains. What little remains is largely overlooked in the religious ritual and confusion. Find the essence of my teachings and give it back to the world. That is how you can help. Will you do this?"

Although I had no idea how I would possibly accomplish this task, there was a deep, palpable feeling of Rightness, so I promised that I would. That was my last dream of Jesus and the beginning of a lifelong quest.

~Chapter 2~
The Search

My search began with the Bible, but because I had a learning disorder, I couldn't read it well enough to really understand it. I was frustrated by not having the means to understand the sources available to me. I was in special education classes in school, but they were not helping me learn to read.

I attended church the few times that my grandparents visited, but always the sermons were negative. I felt that church was not the place for me. Eventually I realized there were no teachers to give me the answers, no books that held the truth I sought. I was dead in the water from step one. Still, I wanted someone to help me.

At the age of 12 I had a strong desire to practice karate. I wasn't very good at it at the time, but the teacher was a kind and honorable man. In retrospect, his technique probably wasn't particularly special, but his focus on teaching us to build strong character, to have integrity and courage, was the nourishment that I craved. I became engrossed in karate training. I walked around my parents' ranch, kicking and punching at all manner of imaginary opponents. I must have been a constant source of entertainment for anyone who took the time to notice.

When I was old enough, my mother began paying me for doing such chores as cleaning the horse paddocks. There were usually a dozen to 20 horses on the property at any given time for boarding and training, so cleaning all of the paddocks was very time consuming. And like any kid, I tended to daydream through work.

For safety reasons, my mother demanded that I move the horse out of its corral and into a holding area before I began mucking. One day, I decided to skip this step to save time. I had my back to the horse while cleaning, fading in and out of daydream as usual. Suddenly there was an intense pressure at the back of my head, and without any conscious decision on my part, my body moved quickly aside as if it had a mind of its own. A horse's hoof flew past me. The horse tried to kick me in the back of the head. I turned and whacked it with my plastic rake until it was backed into a corner and showing submission. After the horse calmed down, I led it to the holding area as I should have done to begin with, then I returned to my duties.

There was a tremendous energy in my body, and a profound calm accompanied my work. A few minutes later, I felt a pulling sensation from above. My eyes were drawn to a single cloud, high in the sky, directly overhead. My body filled with light as my consciousness was pulled up into the cloud.

I found myself just inside the entrance of a hotel conference room. I instinctively knew it was a vision of things to come. There was a man on stage teaching a standing-room crowd about spirituality, the purpose of life, and how to be truly free. He did not look like a pastor or priest or any other type of clergyman, yet he was altogether holy, not in the way he physically appeared but in the presence that emanated from his very being. An unconditioned love invisibly pervaded the room, giving as great or greater a lesson than the words he spoke. Although people could not see this love, they could feel it. This great teacher had an aura about him which was so true, pure, and powerful that just to be near him was enlightening and healing. It was then I realized that this was my future. Suddenly I was back in my body, filled with bliss. I loved that great teacher, and I knew this was to be my future, but how I would get there I had no idea.

This vision was incredibly inspiring, but it also reminded me of my promise to Jesus. I was a fairly weak child and not very good at anything apart from running. I could run like the wind, but I knew that running wasn't going to help me keep my promise. I feared that I would disappoint Jesus, myself, and anyone who needed the teachings. If I failed, my life would not be worth living, I thought. In retrospect, it was a tremendous pressure for a child to bear.

These were very frustrating times in my life, because I had no spiritual mentors. My only mentor was my karate instructor, but I felt he would not understand my situation, so I never mentioned it to him. Shortly after that vision, my karate instructor moved away and was replaced by another instructor who was far less noble. I continued with karate for a while, but the entire atmosphere of the dojo changed for the worse once Peter Sensei left, and it was no longer a pleasant place to be, so I quietly dropped out.

~Chapter 3~
Personal Apocalypse

Apocalypse is a hot-button word in society, and one that most people misunderstand. When we think of apocalypse we think of total destruction, but what we fail to see is its other aspect, which is revelation. It entails breaking everything down to such an extent that the only thing left is truth. This is exactly what happened to my life as events occurred to destroy my world and bring me to the precipice of suicide.

As I mentioned previously, I was in special education in elementary school due to a learning disorder. I was put in a trailer behind the school to be with other such students. We were not taught how to read but just given busy work. There was a feeling that the teacher did not believe in us, and I mistakenly took that feeling to heart. Most of the children in that class were frustrated and rebellious and, of course, troublemakers, and though I was with them, they were not my friends.

Fortunately, I had become good friends with an older neighborhood boy who had graduated high school several years early and already had his own computer software company. Tim was a strong reader, able to consume about 100 pages of a typical novel in about an hour. He had an entire closet filled from floor to ceiling, back to front, with books he had read. I was in awe of his intellect.

I received a computer one Christmas, and since no one that I knew, apart from Tim, had any computer experience, he and I became good friends. On Friday nights, Tim would always go to the bookstore and buy three or four books to read over the span of the evening. Sometimes, I would stay over at his place on Friday nights to play games on his computer. The one rule on sleepover nights was no sleeping, so I would play video games while Tim read his books. He'd burn through all of them come breakfast time. I, on the other hand, would continue playing video games until it felt like my eyeballs would fall out and roll around on the desk.

Tim often told me of the interesting characters, of the twists and turns in the novels he had read. He read a lot of historical books as well, sharing with me how WWI began with the happenstance assassination of Archduke Franz Ferdinand of Austria, or how the Germans lost WWII thanks to their invasion of Russia as winter set in, and so on. Little by little, I became interested in reading about history, politics, and economics.

Tim, I am sure, knew that I could not read, but he never once mentioned it, which I greatly appreciated. Instead, he ignited my interest by taking me to bookstores, where he would invariably recommend this or that title to me while he made purchases. After repeated bookstore visits, I took the bait. I asked Tim if I could borrow one of his books. He lent one of his favorites, insisting that I keep it for as long as it took me to get through it. I began reading as soon as I got home. I read the first page at least 30 times because each time I was ready to turn the page, I could no longer remember the content. Nonetheless, I kept trying for the better part of a month, forcing my way through the first 10 pages, even though I could not retain anything.

Eventually, I admitted my defeat and asked Tim if I could borrow an easier read. This time, he lent me a twisted horror book about vampires, which was much less challenging and had a lot of sex in it, which is enough to motivate almost any budding teen. I read it a little at a time and was slowly able to understand the story line. This book was the first in a series, so once I finished with it, I borrowed the next and the next until I was done with the series. I was beginning to feel comfortable with reading. As I became more confident, I asked for progressively more challenging books, eventually returning to the first book Tim lent me. This time, I was able to read it comfortably, and my confidence soared.

As I said, Tim had graduated high school several years early. And now that I could read and I had gained some confidence, I became interested in that idea. I was never a very good student, but now that I had some confidence in myself, I wanted a challenge. I wanted to graduate as soon as possible, so I could go to college and thereby pick and choose my own classes and enjoy a more mature student body. I began reading books about war, finding that, in the history of war, a lot can be learned about modern civilization.

Civilization, in the forms it has taken, has been (and remains) based on war and dominance of resources. Cities are unsustainable, having to acquire resources externally. What happens when people outside a city do not want to give of their resources? Some combination of physical, economic, and/or cultural warfare ensues. Centralization of power creates a resource-hungry situation that inevitably brings about domination and warfare in the name of progress. The studies of governance, law, taxation, politics, geopolitics, economics, energy, technology, and so forth, are all corrupt children of centralized power. School prepares children to be cogs in the machine of centralization, not to question the system, so, gradually seeing this, I spent less time on my school studies and much more time on my own.

We lived in California, which has a test called the California High School Proficiency Examination that lets students graduate high school early. All I had to do to get my diploma was pass this test. Tim was sure that I could do it, just as he had a few years earlier, so I gave myself one year to prepare for it. I disregarded my school studies and focused on what really mattered: reading, writing, and to a lesser extent mathematics. During this time, my only social contact was Tim. We'd get together to bowl, play table tennis, billiards, and video games while discussing geopolitics, economics, history, and other such topics.

By and by, Tim moved away, and I found myself alone. During the entire time that I knew Tim, I never once told him of the visions or my promise to Jesus. To him, nothing could exist beyond what the logical mind could define and what science could prove. I knew he would not respect my chosen direction, so I kept quiet. To fill the social void created when Tim moved away, I began training at the dojo again. The new teacher was young and only interested in technique, so I went there more for social purposes than anything else.

About this time my mother hired a new ranch hand, John. Although he was nearly 60 years old, he had a lean, stocky, muscular body. He liked boxing, and I liked the martial arts, so we enjoyed conversation. He was a nice man who often gave me well-meaning if not always wise advice. I really enjoyed having him around. He lived quietly in a trailer behind our barn, his salary a pittance. I assumed he had fallen on hard times and just needed the work even if it didn't pay much. He worked hard and didn't drink, so he was all right by me.

My parents bought me an old Volkswagen Bug on my 16th birthday. One afternoon, I needed to go to the convenience store, and I asked John if he wanted to come along. He agreed, and we enjoyed conversation as we drove. On the way home, I noticed that John had become unusually quiet and that he was paying a little too much attention to the rearview mirror. I looked back and found that a sheriff's squad car was on my tail. Without taking his eyes off the side mirror, John told me to remain calm and drive slowly. The squad car followed us for several long miles, and I was beginning to think that it was nothing when the siren sounded. As I pulled over, John nervously told me that if asked about him I should say that I had just picked him up as a hitchhiker. John was in trouble with the law.

Two deputies came on foot along each side of my car. The one asked for my license and registration while the other took a good look at John. I was informed that I had a taillight out and needed to have it fixed. The officer on my side then leaned in for a long, clear look at John. Surprisingly he said we were free to go, and they returned to their car.

I pulled away, my head in a spin. I demanded that he tell me what he was in trouble for. He said he would only tell me if I promised not to tell anyone. I said I couldn't make that promise if he was involved in any harmful or violent crimes. He said that I should know he would never hurt anyone. He confided that he was an escaped convict, but he assured me that it was nothing serious. He was busted for selling marijuana and justified that it really wasn't dangerous and shouldn't be illegal. He assured me that he didn't do anything unlawful anymore, so I need not worry about it. I promised to keep quiet.

About a month went by without a visit from the sheriff, and I began thinking that they had not recognized John after all. Then one Sunday afternoon, that assumption was shattered when a horde of black cars poured onto our ranch. The property was crawling with what appeared to be thugs, drug dealers, and pimps armed with shotguns, automatic weapons, and pistols. We were terrified. Eventually, several "pimps" addressed us flashing police badges. They calmly told us to remain inside and then peacefully explained the situation.

John was a wanted felon, convicted of cooking up and selling crystal methamphetamine. Crystal is a hard drug and definitely harmful. The police had been monitoring John's criminal activities, through undercover agents, waiting for the right time to spring their trap. He was using the small trailer to cook up the drug and then having a friend come over on occasion to pick up and distribute it.

I asked if I could go to the trailer to confirm his illicit activities for myself. As I neared the trailer, the police were hauling John's girlfriend away. I learned that, earlier, they captured John at a small private airstrip, so we never had a chance to see him again, thankfully. I peeked into the trailer and saw his setup. John was a drug dealer. I couldn't believe I fell for his lie.

I was glad they caught John, but I felt guilty for not telling my parents that John was an escaped convict when I should have. I felt that I had been an accomplice to John's illicit activities, enabling him to produce his poison. Had they wanted to, the police could have legally seized my parents' property, and it would have been my fault. I fell into a silent depression, having lost trust in myself. Unbeknownst to me at that time, an undercover officer who had been posing as a drug dealer had made the point of observing my parents for several months leading up to the sting, and so he knew that my parents had no knowledge of the illicit activities.

Just about this time I took the California High School Proficiency Examination, passed it, and earned my diploma. I stopped going to school in the middle of my 11th-grade year. I decided to attend a local college and later transfer to a university to save money. While waiting for my first semester to begin, I worked for my mother on the ranch, doing the work that John used to do. I changed my college plans from full-time to part-time until we found someone suitable to replace me. I was fearful that we would end up with another deadbeat employee. I gave up my plans of transferring quickly to a four-year school. I graduated high school early in hopes of speeding my education only to end up being back in the slow lane. I had no faith in myself, I had no friends, and my dreams were slipping through my fingers. I told no one.

I continued training at the dojo, where I was to test for the rank of brown belt in karate, the rank just below black belt. Karate tests at that dojo typically lasted four or five hours. The test began in the morning and continued nonstop until about 3 p.m. We did countless pushups, sit-ups, and squats, and we ran to exhaustion, only then to be tested on technique. Finally, we had to spar against the black belt students. After the sparring was finished, the instructor had the students wait in the dressing room while he did the next activity privately with one student at a time. There was a crackling sound like a Taser and then a scream. After a minute, another student was taken out of the dressing room to be tased. By the time my turn arrived, I had firmly decided not to be fearful. I was going to take the shock without thought or hesitation; I knew that it would not do permanent damage.

I stood in front of my fellow students, the instructor approaching, the blue light of the Taser crackling. He asked me to stand still and prepare to be tased. "Okay, I am ready," I said, not allowing my mind to think about it. He put the Taser toward my arm, but I continued staring into the distance as if he were not there. The crackle sounded, but he did not touch me with it.

It was all an act to test our emotional reactions. He seemed surprised that I didn't flinch or otherwise show any fear. He retrieved a large-caliber revolver from his office. He told me to take the gun, aim it at my head and pull the trigger. Immediately, without any thought, I took the gun, and without checking to see if it was loaded, aimed it at my head and squeezed what I thought was the trigger – but the trigger would not budge. I quickly released the safety and returned the muzzle to my head. Washed with a pallor, the instructor quickly pulled the pistol from my grasp.

He showed me that the trigger had been removed, so there was no way for me to shoot myself. He admonished that we should never blindly follow orders, no matter who gives them, and that I should have checked to see whether the gun was loaded before handling it. Most importantly, he said that I should never try to kill myself. These were all important lessons, but I felt humiliated, I broke down in tears feeling exposed. You see, secretly, I had hoped that the gun was loaded — or at least I didn't care whether it was. In that moment, I knew I was suicidal, and I felt that everyone else knew it too.

Although I passed the test and received my new rank, I was in no way happy about it. I felt like a total failure. No. I *knew* I was a total failure. I stopped going to the dojo. I guess I should have known of my suicidal tendencies earlier, but I had been in denial.

I got caught up with a bad element, drinking alcohol and smoking marijuana to escape from myself. My life was a constant performance because I pretended to be what I was not in order to fit in. I couldn't tell anyone of the visions or my true goals, and the further I strayed from my dreams, the more I hated myself. One summer afternoon I locked myself in my bedroom and admitted my suicidal tendencies. I could find nothing of myself that was worth redeeming. To stay in the world any longer was a waste of resources because I had nothing to offer. I was just another mouth to feed, and there was no hope for me.

After I finished preparing for my suicide, letter to family written and method set, I sat down on the floor for a moment just to be. Ironically, knowing that I no longer had a future or past to worry about was a huge relief. I had nothing to fear, nothing to become. There was no longer any need to pretend that I was someone else.

I relaxed and a profound peace enveloped me. My eyes were drawn to the rays of light pouring through the window. I witnessed something that I had never noticed before: the dazzling display as rays of light intersected with particles of dust floating in the air. It appeared as if there were tiny angels of brilliant light. It amazed me that I had lived for 17 years, yet I had never noticed this amazingly divine phenomenon before.

Suddenly, my body surged, and a voice rang through it, my chest feeling like a speaker: "You can change your life. You can stop spending time with those who are selfish and negative, who don't really care about you. You can stop drinking and smoking. You can find friends who are working for something positive, who have a purpose in life that you respect. You can go to college even if only part-time. Make your life full of positive purpose. You are free to do what you feel is right. Do what you want to do, and be yourself."

It felt as if an angel had spoken through my body. The voice was so clear and full of Rightness that I trusted it completely. Had it been my own thought or the advice of a person, I am sure I would have rejected it. But now I knew I could do whatever I set my mind to if I just kept at it positively.

There was a power there that transformed me in an instant. The paralyzing effects of doubt and self-consciousness ended in that moment. It's not that I no longer felt doubt, but doubt no longer had any sway over my decisions and actions. My only concern moving forward was doing what felt right. It was such a partition in my life that, looking back on it now, it feels as if I have lived two lives, a negative life of self-consciousness, fear, and doubt, and a new life of passion, love, and direction.

I quickly made new friends, but they never seemed to believe the stories I told them of my negative, self-judging, suicidal life before because that was so different from the person that they knew me to be. The change was rapid, but it wasn't all glory. There were times of frustration when I regressed a bit into negative attitudes. But regardless of the difficulties, I had decided to live my life with purpose — fearlessly and passionately, without regret.

Several years went by during which I focused on preparing for a profession. I wanted to be a psychiatrist in order to help people the way that angelic voice had helped me. During this time, there were occasional spiritual communications, but, for the most part, my life was fairly typical for a college student. I had a girlfriend, and I was learning what it meant to be in love and to have a relationship. I was now living a passionate life and no longer wishing for death.

~Chapter 4~
Back on the Path

A few years later I found myself dissatisfied with the direction I was taking in school. Although I had learned a lot from college, I realized that I was spinning my wheels in some respects. I had formulated the plan to be a psychiatrist in hopes that someday I could do for others what that divine voice had done for me on my day of planned suicide. But after some study I realized, at least for me, that psychiatry was not the right path, so I put college on hold and began looking for work.

I got a job offer in another state, and I took it as an opportunity to leave everything behind and start anew. I entered my new job with nothing but the passion for working hard and learning something in the process. I was excited about moving to Georgia because I had never been to that part of the country.

While in Georgia, I was invited to attend a multilevel marketing meeting in Charlotte, North Carolina. The idea that I had to help others succeed in order to succeed myself in the business sounded intriguing, so I accepted the offer.

I didn't have a car, so the couple that invited me agreed to pick me up at the bus station and drive me up from Georgia. A friend dropped me off at the bus station, but after he left, I realized it was the wrong station. The station I needed to be at was over a mile away, and I had to be there in less than 10 minutes. With no other means of transport, I ran, suit and briefcase, on a sweltering summer day.

By the time I arrived at the correct bus station, I was swimming in my suit. I went to the curbside to look for the car that was to pick me up. I was so focused on my search that I hardly noticed the large man who approached me from my right. He asked me if I had any money. Without looking, I answered that I didn't. It was true; I really had no money, only a credit card. He came closer, encroaching on my personal space. "I said, 'Do you have any money? Give me some money now.'"

It was clear that he was in the process of mugging me. I noticed he was holding a knife, tip nearly touching my right rib cage. Due to my martial arts training, I knew that under normal circumstances I could probably handle this guy easily enough, but behind him were two others watching in wait. If I fought them, someone, probably myself, would be seriously injured or killed. I didn't have any energy to fight after my mile jaunt across town. Worse still, I didn't have money to give them, which would have been my ideal choice given the circumstances. There seemed to be no way out of this situation; someone was going to be hurt or killed.

I took a deep breath, expanded my field of vision and relaxed. Suddenly my body filled with energy, and it felt like I was spread over infinity. My mind went totally silent. I turned to him, my left hand very lightly hovering over his arm yet not actually touching him. It was such that were he to stab, his knife would deflect past me harmlessly. I looked straight through his eyes and repeated, "I said 'I – Have – No – Money.'"

His eyes grew wide as he froze for a few seconds, unable to speak. Shaken, he slowly backed away. "It's cool, man ... it's cool." He turned around and subtly shook his head to his friends, who looked away as if nothing had happened. Just then my ride pulled up to the curb. Calmly, I got in the back seat and we drove off, my chauffeurs not realizing what had just happened. Immediately we struck up a good conversation that ranged from life in Georgia, to family, friends, etc. About a half hour later the topic changed to the recent crime uptick in Atlanta Georgia. This reminded me of the attempted mugging. I was so relaxed from the experience that I had forgotten it. Seeing as we were discussing crime, I used this opportunity to tell them about the mugging attempt, but they clearly didn't believe me, so rather than arguing with them, I let it drop.

As it turned out the attempted mugging was only the beginning of the adventures in store for that weekend. The multilevel marketing meeting was so popular that it took place in a sports stadium. When we entered the stadium, I noticed that off to the right, raffle tickets were being sold. I have never liked lotteries or raffles, so I just ignored it and walked past. But as I passed there was a very strong feeling coming from the raffle area as if someone were pulling on the back of my collar.

Whenever this feeling occurred it always meant something miraculous was about to happen. In the past, if I ignored it, invariably, there was a deep sense of regret, so I surrendered and bought a raffle ticket for a free phone, which I didn't need. I got my ticket, and we took our seats in the bleachers to listen to the day's many speakers talk about "The Business." Nothing else out of the ordinary happened that day.

The next day opened with a prayer session led by a Christian minister. This struck me as odd, as it was immediately followed by prayers to Mammon by top-level sales people. There were thousands of people in the stands, and the speakers were all millionaires who without exception spoke about owning big houses, having luxury and sports cars, and being worth lots of money. The audience seemed to worship these people. I was dumbfounded that they could start out this event with a prayer service about love and light, and then in the next moment be worshiping greed. It was shameless. The speeches went on for hours, and the audience as a whole treated these speakers as if they were saints.

The level of sheer greed was beyond my comprehension. I just couldn't understand why anyone would spend so much time and energy trying to acquire so much stuff. Humans have a limited amount of time and energy, and how we invest that energy determines everything about us, our families, our communities, and ultimately our world. Considering that upon death all of those riches are naught, what is the point? Yes, in order to sustain our physical bodies and put a roof over our heads, we have to be mindful of money, but beyond that ... well, I just didn't get the appeal.

Looking around, I felt that these people were missing something in their hearts. Immediately, I was moved to prayer, a prayer from my soul to theirs. I imagined unconditioned love pouring into their hearts. It was so clear that I could actually see it with my eyes — love displacing the greed and causing it to drain away. The whole stadium was filled with the light of love. I must have been immersed in this prayer for a long time because there were several speeches that had taken place while I was praying, and even a popular 1980s rock band had come onstage and played some of its hit songs – I paid no attention to any of it, so engrossed in prayer was I.

The concert ended with a standing ovation. I stood up too in order to remain incognito. The momentum of my physical body stopped when it reached its full six feet, two inches, but my spirit just kept on rising. It rose halfway out of my body. I looked around and it was as if I were seeing through eyes that were several feet above my head.

The spiritual "eyes" gave me much more information than my physical eyes ever could. Everything glowed with a white light – the floor, the bleachers, even people's clothes. I knew that everything was alive and intelligent in a way that people can't see. Time seemed different, too. In this state, I was able to experience a much greater depth than normal. As the band left the stage, we sat down, and although my spirit descended back into my body, it was still my window of perception.

Onstage, probably 70 yards from me, came the raffle announcer. I looked at him as if through a telescope. I could see inside his right front pants pocket, which contained a folded piece of paper. Just then, a bullet of pure white light shot from the paper and hit me in the forehead, and I saw that my name was written thereon. He reached into his pocket, took out the paper, opened it, and with a strong southern accent said, "The winner of the MCI cordless phone raffle is—" I stood up before he said the name, "— Richard Haight." I had won the raffle, yet I didn't care about the phone. All I cared about was the depth of spirit that had touched me through prayer and what it might imply.

I don't remember anything else of the meeting nor the ride home, so totally engrossed was I in trying to understand the incredible spiritual experiences of that weekend. All I wanted was understanding, and I was going to do whatever it took, go wherever I had to go, in order to get it, so long as it was right by my conscience and led by spirit.

~Chapter 5~
Isness

I knew I had received what it was that brought me to Georgia and that the time had come to move on. The urge to go back to California was so powerful that I gave my notice at work immediately and left as soon as I could. I drove 52 hours straight, meditating the entire time, consuming neither caffeine nor stimulant. I was fueled by spirit.

Almost immediately upon my return to California, I found a group of psychics who were doing healings, readings, channelings, and so on. I wanted to understand the things that were happening to me, and so I joined them in hopes that there was something they had to teach. I met and worked with many psychics, but there was always something about this work that didn't quite sit right for my life. It wasn't until I broke my ankle while preparing for a karate tournament that everything became clear.

As I was helping some friends prepare for a black belt division tournament, I fractured my ankle by checking a kick incorrectly. It didn't hurt, and there was no swelling, so I had no idea that it was broken. We just continued sparring until the tournament contestants were clear on their strategies and tactics. After practice, I drove to the home of a friend, Michaela, who was studying to be a medium. A medium is someone who channels spirits and reads people's futures, etc. We went out to dinner at our favorite Chinese restaurant to talk. Shortly after sitting down, I felt a growing pain in my right ankle. I looked down to see that it had swollen up to twice its normal size. Moving it was excruciatingly painful, and I was unable to put any weight on it. I had previously fractured that same ankle, and it looked and felt exactly the same way it had then.

I went to the doctor's office only to be told that it was a hairline fracture. He explained that is fairly common for people not to feel to break a bone until hours later. It was just a slight break, and casting it would not help much, so I decided to wrap it and use crutches. Little by little, however, the pain got worse, so I visited Jane, a mentor of mine. She had taken me under her wing to protect me from some of the darker elements within the psychic community. Her healing energy was rather powerful, so I was hoping that it would take away the pain enough that I could at least sleep.

Jane, upon seeing my ankle, agreed to help out, so I lay down on her healing table and she began sending energy with her hands. To my surprise, it made the pain much, much worse. I respected her so much that I couldn't ask her to stop for fear of insulting her. Instead, I decided I would try to meditate myself beyond the pain.

As I meditated, I cleared myself of all disharmony. Little by little, I felt as if my spirit was rising up, not out of my body, but rising through spiritual dimensions. I would float up to a certain extent, and, invariably, some negativity within would prevent me from going further, so I had to identify and release it to continue rising. I entered the consciousness of the sun, the solar system, the galaxy, the universe, and beyond. Each has its own identity, feeling, responsibility, knowledge, wisdom, etc.

I went through spirit worlds and what felt like Heaven. Finally I encountered a great void, and just beyond it there was a presence, intelligence, and power so perfect and loving that there are no human words that describe it satisfactorily. It was utterly whole — holy. We humans have a very limited idea of what love is and of what God is, and at that moment my limited perception of both evaporated.

This limitless presence began communicating with me, not in words but in direct understanding. It was as if it put knowledge and experience directly into my consciousness, so information came through purely, beyond the filter of the mind and limitations of words. I inquired, "What are you?" Its answer as best as I can put it into words was, "There is no other."

Indeed, this presence felt to be exactly as it described itself, but I just could not wrap my mind around the next logical implication, that we were one and the same. The all-knowing, all-loving presence was unmistakable, yet what it was saying just did not make sense to my logical mind. How was it possible that it was me if I did not perceive myself as being it?

If I was it, then I too would be omniscient, and since I had no such knowledge, this seemed proof that what it was saying could not be true. So I decided to question this presence further hoping to resolve the ultimate Gordian knot. I started out by asking, "What am I?"

It replied, "No other than I." I was shown how it was always aware of me, even though I was entirely unaware of it up until this moment.

I had read the assertion of Jesus that God is the alpha and the omega, and the words of Buddha that ultimate reality is Oneness, but words are not actuality. The experience is so difficult to adequately explain that words feel like lead dropping from my lips, so heavy and out of place are they.

My mind partially resisted what I was being exposed to, yet somehow I knew it was true. There was a power in this presence that was incomprehensible yet utterly palpable. If this was God, it was entirely beyond the God that I imagined when reading the Bible.

The portrayal of God in most accounts reminds me of a violent, racist, jealous, wrathful, insecure, judgmental man. But there is absolutely no judgment in this presence, nor is there wrath, jealousy, or negativity of any sort. This presence is perfectly forgiving (knowing that there is nothing to forgive), nonjudgmental, and unconditionally loving. Its perfection and love are so enlightening that although it did not judge me, by stark contrast, I could not help but see all of the imbalance in myself. The light of this presence is so pure that anything less than total purity stands glaringly forth, out of place, although my mind was not aware of this until several months later.

My conscience greatly amplified, and I understood that no thought, feeling, or deed of inequity goes unresolved. Until the resolution, the individual cannot truly be at peace, and will continue to experience separation. It's the soul within that constantly draws to the individual the perfect opportunity for balancing through the situations, events, and relationships of life. Our attitude toward these things either binds or frees us.

Because the word God carries with it so many negative associations, and since this presence is beyond the binds of all definition, the word God just felt inadequate to me. I tried to come up with a term that more accurately portrayed its limitlessness. The best one I could come up with was the least defined. It simply *is* with no qualifiers, and so I began calling it Isness for lack of a better term.

Isness unconditionally forgives all things instantly. Even the evilest individual is fully and completely loved by this presence. Although it's able to perceive all universes, it's not bound by anything. There is no fear, only total harmony and understanding.

To be one with Isness became my goal. The feeling is summed up well in The New Testament: "Therefore you shall be perfect, just as your Father in heaven is perfect." I knew that this was possible for all, but I wondered how it was possible for my mind to create separation, negativity, and disharmony, so I asked, "How is it that I perceive myself as different from you? How is it that I perceive myself as being imperfect? How is it that I can perceive imperfection at all?" My attention was directed to what appeared as a giant nebula, or star forming region of space. When I focused on that region, it was clear to me that it was really a clouded mind surrounded by darkness. It had a curious, playful nature, yet it seemed ignorant of its identity and was immersed in the undirected play of self-discovery like that of a young child. From this curiosity countless universes birth, expand, contract, and extinguish, only to birth again and repeat the process with a slightly different angle on things. There were uncountable universes of many different natures, some similar to our own and many not, seeming to be of different dimensionality.

I was shown countless billions or trillions of years in an instant. In all of these universes, ignorance of Isness and the desire to define the self is common. But as deeply engrossed as this clouded mind was in its play, it was never for a moment actually outside of or separated from Isness. It was merely in a playful dream of otherness. The idea of the individual self is, according to Isness, not ultimately true.

I remained consciously aware of Isness for several days. I understood that I and others like myself serve as ambassadors helping those who are ready to wake from the dream of self-identification/otherness to the realization of Isness. It also became clear to me that those who are not palpably aware of and fully tuned to Isness are unstable and bound to experience great disharmony.

After the Isness inspirience (inspirience is my word for any unconditioned experience; its roots are inspire and experience), I found myself in a depression for several years.

I realized how selfish, judgmental, prideful, arrogant, small-minded, and hypocritical I was compared to Isness. All of my darkness was so obvious that I couldn't hide it away anymore, which is what I had been doing unconsciously to some extent all of my life. Since I didn't know how to cleanse myself, there was nothing I could do about this depression until it wore away with time. This may be one reason that very few people have consciously encountered Isness. Could it be that we are unconsciously avoiding realization of Isness for fear of what will be exposed?

Understanding the Isness inspirience became my sole purpose in life. I spent the next few months living with my parents in the mountains while my leg healed. I used this time to begin digesting what Isness had shown me. Mostly I just ached to return to that consciousness, but I couldn't. This feeling haunted me for years but I didn't know how to bridge the gap between the concept of the self and Isness, even though intellectually I understood that there is no separation. Having no way to bridge that gap, I felt frustration beyond measure. So I prayed for an answer.

Several years later, the answer came in a dream. I was in an elevator with a group of strangers going up a skyscraper. About halfway up the building, between floors, the elevator suddenly jolted to a halt. All the passengers were surprised, their eyes betraying their nervousness. Something snapped and the elevator jolted again. Another snap and we were in freefall, the floor numbers counting down in a blur as we sped toward the ground. Everyone was in a blind panic, screaming. Although I knew this was the end of my life, I had no fear. Instead, a great appreciation for life, the good and the bad, welled up within, for I had learned from all of it. I prayed from my heart, "Thank You," and I stretched out my arms to embrace my last moment on Earth. At that moment the elevator began to slow, and just before hitting the ground floor it smoothly stopped.

I awoke in deep thankfulness, knowing that this was the way to live with Isness. I was free of my fear of death and my desire to escape "the prison of the body." I would embrace the present moment fully and with passion, because it's only through the present moment that we truly live.

All of which is a lot easier said than done. It's an ongoing process wherein relaxed persistence pays dividends. We will have our ups and downs, regardless of who we are. When we fall, we peel ourselves off the asphalt and get back up. If we need to cry, then we cry. And when we're ready, we get back up and move forward again.

~Chapter 6~
Land of the Rising Sun

While digesting the teachings of Isness over the next few years, I got a stable job and worked a regular schedule. I met a woman from the psychic community, Kate, who was interested in learning about the Isness inspirience to discover what wisdom might be hidden there. She supported my search with her interest, which helped me to feel more comfortable with sharing the information. I loved the opportunity to elucidate on Isness and its implications. Although I cannot say that I was very successful in my attempts then to pass on the information, Kate was a wonderful cheerleader and supporter, which helped me in ways beyond description.

One day another martial artist asked which martial art I thought was the most effective, a question that I normally would not answer, but before I knew it out of my mouth came, "Aiki." It was not my opinion, but my mouth said it anyway. It was not me speaking, but it felt right. I didn't really know the meaning of the word, but I was familiar with aikido. I went in search of an instructor but was unable to find one that felt right for me. I saw a video of a martial arts instructor from Japan who taught a style called Daito-Ryu Aikijujutsu, the predecessor of aikido. In his Daito-Ryu school, the focus of the training was on aiki, a core principle of his art. In the video, that man could throw people effortlessly and with almost no movement whatsoever. It looked fake, but his movement had a flow and stability about it that was undeniable. Listening to this instructor explain his art, I could feel no deceit. I felt pulled to go to Japan to meet this man, so I quit my job and was on a plane within a few weeks.

I arrived early with a translator at the training hall, a local sports center similar to the YMCA but with mats for martial arts training. We met with the instructor before class, and over a light meal, during which he told us that his art had a long tradition and that he was one of the few instructors teaching it openly. He welcomed us to observe training that night; if I were interested after observing, I was welcome to become a member.

After the meal, he changed into his training attire, and the lesson began. We watched from the edge of the mats as this master threw students of all sizes around effortlessly. We were not the only incredulous observers that night. It just so happened that a reporter from a Japanese martial arts magazine was there to take photos for an article. Judging by the quizzical look on his face, he too was not sure what he was seeing.

Later he politely told the instructor that he could not understand why the students were falling down so easily. He confided that he was not sure that the techniques were real. He said that he was a sixth-degree judo black belt and that he wanted to feel the techniques for himself to verify the art. He said that he did not want to write an article on something that was not authentic.

What happened next was absolutely astounding, not just to us, but to the journalist as well. The instructor held out his right arm and told the man to grab him hard in an arresting fashion. The judo man latched onto the old man's arm and cranked down, causing the instructor to bend at the waist. The instructor asked if the man was ready, and in reply he was given the okay. The next moment the judoist was flat on his back while the old man stood upright, as relaxed as if he had just consumed a glass of wine.

The judo man got up, shook his head in disbelief, and asked if he could try again, saying that he was not ready the first time. The old man smiled and extended his arm again, allowing for the exact same hold and telling the judoist not to hold back. The judoist bore down on the arm and fixed his stance for stability. The old man said, "On the count of three I will start the technique. Are you ready? One ... two ... three ...." Instantly the man was flattened, hitting the back of his head firmly on the mat. A little dazed, he got up slowly, bowed deeply, and thanked the instructor.

Not realizing that the instructor did not normally allow outsiders to test him in this way, I asked if I might be allowed to try. I was a confident, strong, young man, and I was not going to allow myself to be fooled. The instructor agreed to demonstrate the exact same technique with me. I was flattened. Once I got up, he held out his index finger and told me to grab it. As soon as I latched on, I was sent flipping heels over head. As I was getting up, he walked briskly back to his changing room.

I joined the dojo that night, attending every training session thereafter, but before long an old back injury re-emerged, interrupting my ability to train. When I was 17, I was struck by a runaway horse, the collision compressing my spine like an accordion. After the injury, I wasn't able to train in martial arts as energetically as I had in the past. I wanted to fight in full-contact tournaments, but hard training would always cause my back to go out, preventing further training for at least several weeks. Strength training became impossible. I hoped aiki training wouldn't bother my back, but after taking a bad fall, I found myself unable to walk without severe pain. I was no longer able to train, so although I continued to attend class, I did so only as an observer.

One day, while observing training, my eyes were pulled to the entrance of the dojo as another student came through the door. He seemed to be glowing with a faint light. I went to him and asked what he had been doing to cause such a glow. He was surprised at my comment and told me that he had just received a type of physical therapy called sotai-ho. He gave me the business card of the practitioner, and I called immediately to set up an appointment.

Although that therapy didn't fix my back problem, it did relieve the pain a great deal and gave me a much greater range of motion. I was able to train again, which was my main goal. I also knew that I needed to take lessons from that man, so I became a private student.

A few years later I received my practitioner's license in sotai-ho and opened up my own clinic, operating out of my house in Tokyo. Through my practice, I found that this therapy could help a great many things, and I decided I wanted to find a way to expand its effects to help with an even greater range of ailments. I prayed for wisdom, but I had to wait for the answer.

~Chapter 7~
The Quest

About a year later I felt a strong pull to vision quest, something I learned about during wilderness awareness and survival training. Nearly every "primitive" culture consciously recognizes the value of spiritual training and has or had some form of vision quest. The ancient Japanese, for example, would go into caves and sit alone while fasting in the dark, seeking understanding. The Aborigines of Australia would set out alone for a month walking in the wilderness in hopes of gaining understanding. The native peoples of North America sat alone in the wilderness without food or water for a certain period of days to await revelation. In the *New Testament*, it's written that Jesus spent 40 days fasting alone in the desert. The forms may vary, but the intent is the same.

My first vision quest took place deep in the pine barrens, a flat, sandy forest of pine, oak, and blueberry on the east coast of the United States. There was a group of more than 70 people from all over the country assembled for questing. We spent a few days tenting there to be instructed on the vision quest process and to prepare our personal quest locations.

We all spread out from a long, main trail to find our individual quest locations. I was pulled quite far away from the trail into a thickly brushed area that was not logically "ideal" as it had no substantial shade trees to ward off the hot August sun. Also, because there was no clear path leading to it and it was so far out, after several days without food and becoming lightheaded, I might have trouble finding my way back to the main trail. I didn't want any distractions, and the spot was about as bland a place as could be found. One of the quest helpers advised against this location due to its remoteness and rough terrain, but the feeling of Rightness was so strong that I sided with the feeling, accepting whatever difficulties it might entail. I marked the center of my vision quest circle and then used a string connected to the center, pulled taut to walk around while scuffing the ground to mark the perimeter. Then I cleared out the brush and leaves from the circle. Finally, I dug a small hole a short distance from the circle to use as a latrine. I would spend the next four days and nights inside the larger circle, leaving only to use the latrine and to mark the main trail every morning, thus letting the vision quest helpers know all was well. This circle was to be my life.

The first day of the vision quest was exceedingly hot, with direct sun beating down on me relentlessly. I had one little pine tree that stood not much taller than I for shade. I spent the day like the hand of a clock following the small shadow of that little tree. To make matters worse, the sunshine on my water jugs made the water taste like plastic. There weren't any particularly exciting revelations that day, which was somewhat disappointing; nevertheless, almost all 20 of the pressing questions that I had prepared for myself were resolved by midday. Most of the things that I had thought were important turned out not to be, so the majority of my questions were rendered irrelevant. I realized that many of my priorities had been askew. With that insight, I had much less to worry about.

Despite the correction in my priorities, I still had a lot to challenge me. The same annoying thoughts and feelings went round and round, like flies that just won't stop landing on your face. In modern society, a person wouldn't even notice these thoughts because we unconsciously avoid them by turning on the TV, listening to music, surfing the Internet, striking up a conversation, or otherwise keeping ourselves busied. Always there is something to distract oneself from the fly.

The night sky was full of stars, and I spent many hours gazing at the universe as I tried to quiet my mind. Even the mosquitoes that swarmed and harassed me were less bothersome than the buzzing of my own thoughts. I had a tarp with me for protection in the event of rain. I rolled myself up in the tarp and tried to seal off any entryways to keep the mosquitoes at bay. It more or less worked, but nothing would stop the bug in my head from buzzing on.

The next morning's greeting was drizzle, and it continued, nonstop, for two days and nights. Because of the lack of variety, I found myself hoping for the scorching sun again. The sheer monotony of the constant drizzle was mind-numbingly dull, but the fly in my mind never missed a beat.

Around noon the third day, my mind began to quiet. There would be long periods of silence followed by more noise. That afternoon the clouds began to clear, making way for a beautifully rejuvenating sunset. I climbed that poor little shade tree, causing it to bend over sideways, just so I could get a clear view of the sun setting. Having all forms of entertainment and distraction removed from one's life, one really starts to appreciate the simple things. I could fully understand how a person kept in solitary confinement aches for the opportunity to walk outside and see the sky. I promised myself that I would take the time to notice simple beauty every day.

By that evening my mind had quieted, and I thought I was over the hump, but after the sun went down a wave of frustration and annoyance came over me. I was boiling over with a disharmonious feeling in my body that had no apparent cause. I asked myself, "Why am I so pissed off!?!" To my surprise, I yelled, "Because I am fucking hungry." And with that the frustration faded away, as did the hunger.

That night I slept sporadically, waking to the feeling of a dark presence watching me from just outside my circle. I had a flashlight with me which I shone in the direction of the presence, but nothing was there. I knew if it was anything, it was not physical. After I observed the area for a while, the feeling would go away, but it would return as soon as I fell asleep. I went into a meditation and projected a feeling of love and warmth to the entire area. It felt right, so I expanded the feeling to the entire forest, and then the state, and the entire country and the planet. It just grew and grew, and there was nothing that was excluded from it. Even Satan, if he exists, was welcomed into this light. I fell into a deep sleep, feeling safe and secure.

The next day was an undulation between the light and dark sides of the spirit. I would be in a loving, clear space where it felt as if a light shone through me to the universe, which would then fade into a feeling of tension and anxiety. The anxiety was so intense that I had to stomp it out while walking around my circle, and when the anxiety disappeared, I'd be back in the light once more. Again and again this cycle repeated as I purged. I slept in short, seemingly random spurts throughout the day and night without any dreams.

I awoke early to a beautiful sunrise on the last day. This was the morning that we were supposed to leave our quest circles – the quest was over. I had spent four days wishing it to be finished, but now that it was actually over, I didn't want to leave. I had finally reached a point of sublime silence, where I felt totally connected to my environment. It felt as if the earth, the plants, and the animals were my family. They had supported me through an important spiritual endeavor, and, finally, we could communicate clearly. I felt I could communicate with trees more easily than I could with people because there wasn't any sense of ego or separation. After hanging out with my new family for another hour, I decided to leave before someone came looking for me as was the policy. The vision quest was officially over, but it never really ends.

I stayed in the forest, camping for several more weeks before heading back to the hustle and bustle of Tokyo. I knew I needed to find a new martial arts teacher for my path to continue unfolding properly. I was pulled to another instructor of the same art, who was also a teacher of the sword and short staff. I took up the training in earnest, embracing all of the arts he taught. This instructor taught very conscientiously, giving a little private time to each student every lesson, which I felt was extremely beneficial.

I was a bit frustrated that none of my techniques worked on his students. I was already a second-degree black belt, but my training was useless. I decided I needed to completely give up any ideas about the art and start afresh. I knew nothing.

~Chapter 8~
The Amazon

As a result of the vision quest, I knew I needed to take a trip into the jungle and spend some time with a tribe. I didn't know when, where, or why, but I knew at some point I needed to learn directly from people living close to the earth. I did not know what it was I was to be taught; I only knew I needed to go. Four years later I joined an eco-tour to Ecuador. It was a 10-day tour starting in the Andes, going through the mystical cloud forests and descending to the Amazon Basin for a five-day immersion into a small village. I landed in Quito in late July and met up with the tour group, 13 wonderful people from all over the world. We spent several days in the Andes, where we met a Quechuan shaman who lived in a valley between two huge volcanoes. He invited us to take part in a cleansing ceremony before heading down the Andes to enter the jungle.

For the ceremony we took off our clothes and stood in a dungeonlike room beneath a brick house. The shaman and his son wiped our bodies and hair with various herbs. They used stones and eggs to remove darkness from us. They even blew flames from their rum-filled mouths at us from a safe distance; the energy and warmth felt surprisingly good. Despite the strangeness of it all, every single one of us said we felt a lot better for having participated. Unanimously, we agreed that our bodies felt lighter and clearer.

After the ceremony we were famished, so we headed to a restaurant. We had been warned not to drink nonbottled water in Ecuador due to diarrhea-causing bacteria in the country's water supply. Not thinking, I ate the salad. In retrospect, I realized, it was certainly washed in tap water. By the next day, I was exploding out both ends, and for three days I was unable to eat anything. Despite my intestinal plight, I was still excited about what was to come.

We wound our way down the Andes to a town called Shell (after the company that built it) that stood at the edge of the rain forest. The Achuar tribe owned a small hangar there with several small, prop-driven planes used to transport people to their jungle village. We boarded our respective planes, piloted by trained Achuar tribesmen, and within minutes began our adventure in the sky.

Our pilot flew high over the forest, following a meandering river east, the jungle below us stretching to the horizon in every direction. As we neared the pilot's tribal runway, he looked back at us with a grin, then suddenly, we were in a sharp dive for the river. He leveled off just above the river, the wingtips nearly skimming as he banked to follow the water's flow. My neighbor, a gregarious Australian woman, reached over and grabbed my arm stiffly as I smiled from ear to ear.

Finally, off to our left, a muddy airstrip running parallel to the river appeared. Achuar children who came to watch us land lined both sides of the runway. The moment we splashed onto the runway, the windows streaked with mud. The little boys ran and hid, leaving behind only little girls, the mighty warriors. We climbed out of the plane, scampered off the runway, and blessed the earth.

The second plane came in, and we lined up along the runway like the Achuar children to watch. After the new arrivals reacquainted themselves with the earth, we were led down to the riverbank, where a couple of motored canoes awaited us. We boarded and headed down the river to our final destination, a small lake surrounded by Achuar-style huts for eco-tourists. Each hut was equipped with a bed, a shower, and mosquito netting.

Over the next several days we took hikes through the forest to learn about its ecosystem, the Achuar guide teaching us about various flora and fauna and how each had its place. We learned what was edible and what was medicinal. While the rain forest holds untold potential for beneficial medicines yet to be discovered, surprisingly many plants and trees there are inedible to humans. We were also surprised to learn that living in the jungle required some degree of farming, which was the responsibility of women. Men were responsible for fishing, hunting, and building structures as well as protecting the tribe. Women worked harder on a daily basis, but the men had a much more dangerous life.

On the second morning we hiked deep into the jungle; we used the river to come back in the afternoon. We floated for hours on a slow, meandering tributary that fed into the Amazon River. There were kayaks for those who wished, but many of us just swam. We saw a variety of wildlife: river dolphins, red monkeys, large turtles, and sloth. Anacondas, caimans, and piranha inhabit the river, but we weren't worried much about them with our Achuar guides keeping a lookout. Reputedly there is a little fish that swims up the urethra of unwary individuals who urinate while in the water. Its fin-bones can't bend backward, and once it enters the urethra, the bones get lodged in the passage's walls, leaving the tiny fish stuck in there. It's supposed to be extremely painful and to require surgery to remove. We didn't know whether the stories were true, but we held it.

By the time we were back to our village that evening, we were famished and exhausted. As we enjoyed our Achuar meal of piranha and mashed cassava, we were informed that we had been invited to join in a traditional ceremony by a neighboring tribal shaman. The Achuar and many other tribes typically practice the consumption of an herbal concoction for the purpose of having visions. As I had once used substances to escape from myself, I did not consider them to be of any positive use on a spiritual path. Despite these reservations I felt strongly pulled to take part in the ceremony, and I knew I was about to have an extremely important revelation.

Our group leader instructed us on what this ceremony entails. We would be offered a medicine called natem, a concoction of visionary plants that would send us on a spiritual journey. Each individual would be taught their own personal lessons during their journey. We would receive what we needed, which is often not what we want. We were admonished not to fear or resist, as that could cause a very negative experience. The natem, they said would not alter our sense of self or our thinking. It would tune us to the Godhead, which would instruct us. We were free to accept or reject any teaching after the journey was over, but during the experience we should remain open. After the ceremony we would have time to journal, consider, and make our own decisions regarding the lessons received. At this point everyone who wished to imbibe natem began fasting. The ceremony would take place the following evening.

We left the next afternoon for a silent, prayerful, three-hour hike to the shaman's village. As we neared the village, we took about 30 minutes for solo meditation. We spread out, finding sit-spots where we would meditate and each of us would construct a list of questions to be answered through the ceremony. I constructed my questions and knew that this vision would give me guidance for my life's mission.

After the meditation we continued our trek, and soon we came to a creek with deep walls and a steady flow. A felled tree lay across the waterway and gave access to the far banks, where an apparently amused Achuar man in a loincloth stood and silently watched us. One by one, our guide led us across the creek. Once across, we continued through a small valley and up a hill to a village atop a plateau overlooking a vast Amazon tributary.

The locals greeted us and told us we could set up our tents near their gardens, a bit away from the main tribal huts. By the time we were done setting up, we had another meeting to further instruct us on the approaching ceremony. We decided who was going to receive the natem and who was going to help. The helpers assist journeyers to a secure place in the forest, ensuring safety during the ceremony as well as a safe return.

From a high cliff we looked out over the vast forest, beyond a river that was easily several hundred yards wide, to the horizon as the sun bade us farewell for the night. We remained in silent reverence, awaiting the onset of the ceremony. About a half hour later, when it was dark enough, we were led to the shaman's hut and asked to sit on the benches around the rim of the room. Achuar huts are palm-leaf-covered, open-sided structures. They do not have walls, so our backs were to the open air.

The leader of our expedition asked if I would be willing to be the first to take the natem. I agreed and sat at the front of the bench closest to the shaman, who was dressed in traditional attire with an orange, parrot-feathered headband. He was engrossed in a whispering song-prayer, sending his blessings into a neon-orange brew that had been simmering for most of the day. He stirred the natem with affection, and when it was just right he turned and greeted us.

He directed me to sit on a stool in front of him, and he blessed me with a feather. He gazed at me, then filled a large decorated clay bowl with the orange liquid. He handed it to me, telling the translator that I was to drink it down to the last drop without pause.

Receiving the bowl, I had to be careful not to spill it, as it was filled to the brim. We were told that natem is a bitter drink and that we might have trouble getting it down, but it really wasn't so bad. I drank it down as quickly as I could, but my stomach had shrunk thanks to the unexpected four-day fast, which made it a struggle.

After emptying the bowl, I was given water to wash out my mouth. I returned to my bench to await my journey.

From my perch at the front of the bench, I was able to observe the portions that the shaman doled out to everyone. It made no logical sense that most people received considerably less than I had been given, despite the fact that almost everyone outweighed me and had fasted for fewer days. I was pretty sure I was in for a heck of a ride.

After everyone finished receiving their portions, we were told that we should expect the effects to start in about an hour and that the effect would last just about as long. Once the effect began we were to be taken out into the forest by a helper where we could purge and have our vision.

Within fifteen minutes my entire vascular system began to vibrate, my blood feeling like static electricity. Dizziness overtook me, and I told my helper, Larry. He assured me, "You're imagining things. Fifteen minutes is way too quick for effects to begin." I told him I was about to puke, and without further debate he helped me out of the tent. He guided me toward the forest, my arm over his shoulder. My mind spinning and stomach rebelling before we got halfway there, my legs became too wobbly to walk in a straight line. There was no way I could have made that walk without help; I had never been so dizzy and disoriented in my life.

Once at the edge of the forest, I got on my hands and knees to purge. After several powerful contractions I lay down on my back, appreciative of the stable ground cradling my body. I felt a mosquito land on my forehead and spear my third eye, and with that the journey began.

I heard an undulating vibration like that of millions of cicada in chorus. The sound would rise and fall in rhythm, increasing in intensity and tempo as the gap between the peaks narrowed. I could feel the energy rising from the base of my body up to the top of my head. By the time the energy reached the crown of my skull, it was a screaming, high-pitched, frenzy of building pressure, and finally it exploded out of the top of my head as if from a volcano.

The first thing I saw was a small, light-blue butterfly with a dot on each wing that looked like eyes. Then a boldly colored fluorescent lizard flashed before me. Then I found my mind no longer in the forest, but in the heart of the earth. A frighteningly powerful voice addressed me. My lesson had begun.

It began by teaching me the purpose of life on Earth. I was taught of the destruction and renewal to come in the near future. I was taught of the coming of Christ and about how this will lead to a cascading shift in consciousness throughout humanity. I was taught of my mission and given direction with regard to that mission. Humanity is on the verge of an incredible enlightenment, but first the corruption of humanity must be fully exposed.

Conscious light from the center of the galaxy will be bathing the solar system with ever-increasing intensity. And with this light, corruption, greed, and selfishness will collapse upon themselves, consuming everything they touch. Within short order the three pillars of humanity — economy, ecology, and society — will fail. Everything that is based on lies and selfishness will crumble with exposure.

I was shown two possible futures that are to be determined by the attitude humanity takes when things begin to collapse. If people maintain selfish, negative attitudes and resist positive change, the suffering will be an immeasurable Hell on Earth. The human population, as well as most of the flora and fauna of the planet, will be reduced to near-extinction levels. The unbearable suffering of humanity rushed in on me; the horror was beyond words. If, on the other hand, we choose a positive, loving attitude that honors all life and embrace the changes as much as possible, things won't be quite as difficult. Even with this attitude, the suffering will be beyond comprehension just because there is already so much negative momentum. In either case, the population of humans will shrink, after which the remaining population will transition into a truly inspiring, consciousness-affirming way of life. Life on Earth will become much richer after these changes occur. People will live positive, inspired lives in communion with all things. What we now call miracles will be common at this time, and people will feel these miracles are perfectly normal and natural.

Earth is a school and a teacher. Here, you are receiving training the way an athlete receives training. In sports, does the coach baby us in hopes that we will gain skill and ability? No, of course not. The coach puts us in difficult situations, knowing that through hard training we will gain ability and strength. The only question is, are we coachable? In the same way, the earth experience is training. But this training is not to add but instead to strip away all that is false, until there is nothing left to veil realization.

There is no escaping the physical experience until one has realized all that is required for graduation. The death of the body is not an escape; we will return in a new body and experience repeatedly until we graduate. In the event that this planet becomes uninhabitable to us, we will incarnate on another planet that serves the same function.

All experience is earned by the individual; which is to say, there are no accidents. We have created the world into which we are born through past incarnations, just as we are creating the world we will be born into in future incarnations.

We get the experiences that we need for growth. Eventually, the endless striving for pleasure, power, safety, comfort, approval and distraction will no longer satisfy, and that is when we will begin to make optimum use of the training opportunity and thereby realize our true nature, which is harmonious.

There are more people on the planet now who are ready to graduate than have ever been at any one time in the history of the world. I was shown that first one person would graduate and light the way for many. There would be a great enlightenment on Earth.

People with negative, selfish minds, who are unwilling to change perspective will die off and reincarnate elsewhere, and for roughly the next thousand years, this planet will be in a high state of consciousness, where many will graduate the school of the earth. Can you imagine a world in which everyone lives positively, seeking understanding, where Christ/Buddha is not seen as a personality but as a realization that is possible for all? What a beautiful world it would be.

The proper attitude is the key to unfoldment, and a graduate of the school of the earth has mastered right attitude. We must not expect someone else to change us or save us. Each individual needs to walk their own path mindfully and decisively with the intent of opening to Isness at their very core. Walking your own path does not mean that you do not learn from others or that others cannot assist in your process, for this is as it should be. Teachers and guides are beneficial and extremely valuable, depending upon the attitudes of all involved. Learn from them, but do not assume anything; avoid over-reliance on them, and do not worship them.

With right attitude, one will learn a great deal from others while questioning and testing everything within oneself. Most importantly, we will open our hearts to direct learning from Isness. We, as humans, will no longer view the people and things of the world as utilities and resources to be exploited, but will instead tune directly with everything and see the intrinsic value and beauty that is and has always been. We will understand that the harvest is important to the health of the ecosystem if done with the right attitude and in the right way.

I was given instructions as to what I needed to do to prepare for my mission on Earth. By combining the aiki and sotai-ho principles, and by practicing them together as one, my martial arts instructor and I would discover a new art that is at once a path to enlightenment, a therapy art, and a self-defense art. Through this path, a great multitude will graduate the school of the earth.

After the vision was over, Larry led me back to the shaman's hut. He had me lie down on a table where the shaman cleansed my body with a feather and his breath. I was taken outside, where blankets were laid out under the stars. I laid myself down there and gazed up at the stars for hours, until the disorienting effects of natem wore off. I got up, went back to my tent, and slept until morning.

At 4 a.m. I awoke to laughter outside. I climbed out of my tent to see what was going on. Near the shaman's hut was the tribe of Achuar, young and old, in a circle to share their dreams. The Achuar believe that their dreams are not for themselves but are messages from the spirit world to be shared with others. So, every morning they all gather and drink a purging tea, and each person has time to share dreams with the tribe. This tea causes the stomach to bring up anything remaining, so that any undigested matter is purged, which the Achuar say prevents many health issues.

Wanting to be a part of a sharing community like that, I felt a strong desire to join them. But it felt inappropriate, so I went back into my tent and just listened as they laughed and told stories in their local language between purges. I wondered if my ancient ancestors had dream-sharing rituals like this one, and, if so, when and why those rituals were discarded. It seemed to me that this sharing community spirit would help a lot of people who suffer from depression and loneliness.

By mid-morning we returned to our village via canoe, and we used the rest of the day to journal and reflect. That night our group visited another Achuar family living in a different area of the forest to enjoy a meal and be shown their traditional lifestyle and skills. I was still so overwhelmed with the vision that I opted out, remaining in my hut and trying to get a grip on the enormity of what I was shown.

I suppose I was suffering from a bit of post-traumatic stress disorder. What I was shown of the destruction to come and the things I needed to do to prepare for my mission was totally beyond my ability to comprehend. I just didn't know how to handle all of the pressure, and my mind was in overdrive. For the rest of the trip, though I was physically present, I was pulled into myself and out of touch. Many of the group members kindly showed concern, but I was unable to share anything with them because doing so felt inappropriate.

After several years of digesting, I now see that we must be willing to give up falsehoods before any truth can be accepted fully. And I can see that, in our society, few are willing to give up the falsehoods that we cling to. Indeed, we may be in for a rough ride. But I no longer concern myself too much with that, as I can't control other people's attitudes. My main focus is fulfilling my part in the story. I am confident that there are many out there who have received important teachings and are doing all they can to fulfill their path in this epic adventure of life.

~Chapter 9~
Discovering the Path

After returning to Japan I visited my martial arts instructor, Shizen Osaki Sensei, and told him of the vision as it pertained to him and the homework I had been given. Of course, he could have thought me crazy and turned me down, but despite my fear, I told him anyway. I told him that I was to combine martial and therapy training, and that through this combining something new would be born, a simple and clear path to enlightenment. I asked him if he would be willing to go down this path of exploration with me.

To my surprise, he was excited about the idea. Before the Amazon trip, he had a problem knee that was making training difficult. I used sotai-ho to help him recover, so as a result he too became interested in bodywork.

I was shown in the Amazon vision that when I had gone deeply enough down the path of enlightenment there would be an energetic field that would serve to protect against malicious intent. I told Sensei about this effect and also that, at a sufficient level of enlightenment, we would be able to execute the entirety of our martial arts skills without any effort or thought. What this really meant was that meditation would become the core of our training.

We began first with uncovering the meditation by way of practicing sotai-ho on each other. There was a feeling in the body that we discovered after receiving therapy. Eventually we were able to tune to this feeling purely through meditation, and then by using this feeling we could apply therapy to each other without using techniques. In this way, the therapy became technically liberated. It became easy to detect areas of heaviness in the body and use the energetic touch that we had discovered to free up the energy in that area.

We discovered that we could go into this meditation, search our own bodies for low-frequency places, and, merely by lightly intending toward that spot, we found that our bodies would begin to move on their own. It was a spooky feeling at first because the body will move quite dramatically as it naturally stretches itself out and opens up energetic pathways. Previously, my body had moved on its own out of self-defense, but that movement occurred only in extreme situations, such as when the horse tried to kick my head. Now it was happening easily and in nonthreatening situations.

We paid attention to the feeling in the body during these sessions, fed that feeling back into our meditations, and soon a protective field began to emerge around our bodies when in meditation. I noticed only because after meditation, Sensei's body felt to me like it was radiant, and when he asked me to attack him, I couldn't, no matter how I tried; it was as if there were a wall between him and me. It was quite strange, and at first I wondered whether I was just imagining it. He remained in that state, standing there relaxed in front of me, for quite a long time before the effect wore off, but it was a confirmation to me of the Amazon vision.

The next day, we began our training session with meditation, again trying to find that feeling. After some time, Sensei again found it, and I could not attack. I was able to move effortlessly when grabbed and do many techniques that I previously could not do, but the protective field was not there for me. With persistence, we kept at this for several weeks; not once was I able to get it right. Many times, Osaki Sensei succeeded, though. At this point about a year had already passed since the Amazon trip, and the therapy method had evolved tremendously, as did the martial art and the meditation.

We needed to test the field thoroughly but safely, so we used a hard-hat. One of us would put on the helmet and sit on the floor in meditation, and the other would try to hit him on the head with a leather-padded bamboo sword. Sensei was often successful in making the field, yet I did not have a single success until a session some weeks later, when Sensei came in to hit me as hard as he could. He got halfway through his swing, and his foot slammed into the ground propelling his body backward, his sword frozen in midair. He looked like he was in pain. Slowly he put the sword down and sat cross-legged in front of me. "You know," he confided, "I have been thinking you were only stopping your swings because you had brainwashed yourself into believing that you could not hit me. I was getting tired of this useless training and wanted to make you give up, so I swung as hard as I could to discourage you from this kind of training. I wanted to work on something real, but to my amazement this time, when I swung, it was as if I hit a brick wall. My foot hit the ground so hard that my heel hurts. It really worked. I have to admit, it really worked. Let's break for tea. I want to consider this for a bit."

After this success, we practiced more enthusiastically than ever. I started to get a better feel for the meditation and, gradually, had more success with the protective field as well. Session after session brought new discoveries and realizations that kept us busy for hours. We poured our new understanding back into the traditional martial arts as Sensei introduced me to advanced skills in the sword, staff, and open-hand, using the feeling from meditation and therapy as the engine for the traditional forms. My martial arts improved dramatically, and within a few years I was given instructor licenses in the four samurai arts that Sensei had taught at that time.

During my last year in Japan, I stopped work entirely and focused solely on training with Sensei privately. At this time I came every day with some new insight as to how the training needed to go that day for progress. I didn't know how I knew, I just knew. We would start at 1 p.m. and continue training until 6 p.m., break for dinner, and then continue with the regular group classes from 7 p.m. until 9 or 10 p.m. I was training five days a week for at least six hours a day and making rapid progress.

Still, I was often unable to get the protective field effect because I really did not understand what was occurring to cause it, and the more I thought about it the further from it I was. During this training, both Sensei and I regularly became quite exhausted, and after just a few hours, we had to break for coffee and rest. It seemed to me that we were using too much willpower to produce this field. The Amazon vision showed me that this would eventually be an effortless, constant field, but we had yet to discover how. Also, the time and effort it took to activate this field made it highly impractical for a real situation that required immediate response.

I knew there was still more to be discovered, but I also knew that I needed to return to America. It was not logical, but it was clear that it was time for the next step in my journey and that step had to occur in America. In my last six months in Japan I was given the Master's License and, with Sensei's blessing, was sent out to teach. I asked Sensei to help me find a name for this new training method and he suggested shinkaido, which means "open-heart path." Shinkaido is more of a description of the method, rather than a name because through the process of opening the heart our unfoldment occurs.

I moved to a small town in southern Oregon and began teaching a few dedicated individuals. I was new at teaching and was quite nervous about it, so I taught only technically and did not get into the meditation until well over a year after I left Japan. Due to my identification as a teacher, I just could not relax enough to make use of the shinkaido method. Of course, there was the fear of failure and being embarrassed if I was unsuccessful. There was also the fear that the effects would be so startling to people that it might scare them off.

Eventually, I began to relax into the teaching role and introduced a basic meditation that my students could practice for just 10 minutes before each class. My students really seemed to enjoy this meditation, so I incorporated it into regular training. They had been working on a challenging beginning technique and for six months had not been having much success, but after the meditation, they could do the technique easily and without any thought. They were so surprised, and from that point they requested that I make the meditation a primary part of training. Around that time a woman from whom I had been renting space for therapy in a neighboring town became very interested in having me teach meditation classes there. A small group of individuals met there every Tuesday night, and I led them through a basic meditation for an hour, assisting them to move towards greater and greater harmony in their lives. The goal was to have a little more relaxation and awareness each week. They made rapid progress.

About this time, I began mentoring private students several times per week for three hours each session. I found that they gained much more from the concentrated three hours than they would gain from three hours spread over three weeks. So, we set up a full Saturday of training as an experiment. They advanced tremendously from that one day. Whereas before a tiny distraction would cause them to collapse out of meditation, I was then able to use more intense stimulus, and their meditation would hold strong.

I had been away from Japan for two years, and I suddenly felt strongly pulled to visit my teacher there. Three months later I was knocking at my teacher's door. I lived in his dojo for 10 days, during which time we practiced from 7 a.m. until 2 the next morning, living on meditation and coffee. During this time, both Sensei and I regained our footing in the advanced shinkaido method of martial training, as neither of us had been working with it since I left Japan. This intensely concentrated time proved incredibly powerful for me. I gained a deeper awareness of intention, the mind, consciousness and Isness, plus a new confidence to practice in this method and even to teach it.

Once I returned to America, I began holding weekend intensives to get students to deep awareness of inner harmony and keep them there for extended periods of time. Their rate of progress was truly impressive as the presence of each student deepened at an astounding rate. When students had questions for me about the process, I turned the questions back at them, and they were often able to answer themselves through direct insight. A teacher could not have been more pleased.

Before the first intensive I was not sure what I was going to teach, so I made a detailed schedule of activities and teachings. As soon as the students sat down in front of me, my hand reached over and put the plan behind me. All teachings came out spontaneously, and many of the things taught were new to me as well as to the students. It was exhilarating to realize that I did not need to plan anything, and answers would just flow out of my mouth.

Little by little, the students were able to tune more accurately to consciousness, allowing it to flow. Their lives were becoming more enriched and stable. Their minds and emotions became more transparent and mild.

When they lost stability, they realized it quickly and recovered harmony. In only a year's time, they went from near-total energetic instability to a point where they were ready to teach introductory meditation themselves. I could not have hoped for quicker progress.

At the rapid pace that people reach these high states of consciousness and functionality, I can envision individuals spreading throughout the world to pass on this understanding. It will be like a tidal wave of consciousness flowing over the entire planet. My goal is to see a fundamental paradigm shift in human consciousness within four years of keying the period at the end of this sentence. Be open to the possibilities; expecting nothing.

I firmly believe that this realization will end violence on the planet. When individuals understand and prove that love is more powerful than violence, then violence has had its last breath. My hope is that the reader joins me in taking this leap of consciousness as we move out of reactive mind and into conscious unfoldment.

~Part 2~
The Path

The path of spiritual unfoldment is first and foremost a process of resolving to Isness by way of intentional tuning to consciousness. Through the tuning process, identifications that we hold slough away, little by little, like dead skin. We can consider these identifications to be like a dark field surrounding us. With each release of darkness, a little more light is able to shine through, allowing further insight into our true nature.

For this reason the path of unfoldment is unlike any other path in life. It's not a building up of skills and structures but instead is a resolution or dissolution of structure. It's not a becoming but an unbecoming. It's not a complication but a simplification and purification process removing all that we hold onto, for what we hold binds us.

Isness is not something we create or hold on to but instead is most fundamental and, therefore, the default. Thus, even belief systems must be discarded at some point, for all belief systems are of the mind, and it's the mind that veils us from Isness. Through the process of unfoldment the disharmonious structures of mind are unbound, revealing what is most fundamental, and only when the most fundamental is revealed can we embrace everything without holding on to anything.

In Part 2 we'll look at the origins of the universe and its fundamental relationship to the human experience. Then, we will discuss the differences between mind and consciousness, so that we may become aware of when we are tuned to mind and thereby choose to tune to consciousness more often. I'll also introduce a dynamic form of meditation that will serve as a fundamental tool in our tuning to consciousness. Finally, we will go over potential pitfalls regarding the practice of meditation, as well as discover powerful methods for resolving inner disharmony.

~Chapter 10~
Genesis

Imagine you are a formless, curious deity blowing imaginary soap bubbles. A single bubble would represent our universe. Other bubbles would represent other universes. Sometimes, when blowing them, an entire clump of connected bubbles floats out together. This clump of bubbles would represent the multiverse, which contains the sum-total of all universal bubbles combined. The multiverse has more bubbles than could be counted by a supercomputer. And each of its bubbles represents a different reality. Many are just slight variations of one another, but many are so drastically different in content and dimensionality as to be unrecognizable to individuals in other universes.

The source of the multiverse is no different than the source of a human being. The ongoing processes of both are identical, so by understanding the multiverse we can understand the human being, and by understanding the human being we can also understand the multiverse.

"The Eternal Buddha has a three-fold body. There is the aspect of Essence. There is the aspect of Potentiality. There is the aspect of Manifestation."

— The Teachings of Buddha

For practical purposes I name the aspects as Soul/Isness, as spirit/potentiality, and as mind/manifestation. These three are actually one when viewed holistically, but when viewed individually they appear to be separate, unrelated, or even contradictory.

In order to understand the origin of the multiverse, it's important to rid ourselves of notions of time, place, form, and the sense of self and otherness. Avoid initiating cause-and-effect relationships;

instead, consider only the formless moment and that all that is occurring is happening within the moment.

When I was 22 years old, I had what I call the Isness inspirience. During that inspirience, Isness indicated that I was in no way different from it. I felt at a deep level that Isness was indicating truth, but I could not understand how it was possible for me to be Isness and also be ignorant of that fact. Isness is not ignorant, as Isness is aware of all things. Therefore, it seemed to me that my ignorance was proof that I was not Isness.

I asked Isness to show me how it was possible that I could have a separate identity and not be aware of my true nature as Isness. When I questioned how I could be ignorant and still be Isness, I was given the answer, which I did not understand until almost two decades later.

Isness directed my attention to a clouded mind that looked to me like a star-forming region of space called a nebula. I will describe the wordless mental processes of the clouded mind through words to show the commonality with what is happening in the human mind, for they are one and the same in principle.

Imagine there is neither time nor form. There is only the undifferentiated, unbound, vibrant awareness of precisely this instant. Awareness notes, "I don't know what I am." Curiosity wonders, "What am I?" The assumption that is built into the question perturbs and clouds awareness. Curiosity searches into its nature, unaware that there is no true answer to this question, no final conclusion.

As curiosity playfully feels into its nature, attention narrows its focus to isolate definition. Focus collapses awareness into an unconscious, dreamlike state, wherein speculation answers the question, "What am I?" If the answer is, "I am thought", there blows out a bubble of thought, which is an entire universe. But speculation might declare, "I am feelings." There blows out a bubble of emotion, a different universe.

From speculation, countless universal bubbles come into being, of differing natures and dimensionalities, depending upon the premise that speculation goes into. Although these universes are different in many ways, they all have the same core attributes: assumption, self, otherness, time, and disharmony. Thus, each universe is made up of interdependent opposites, like the Chinese yin-yang symbol. In our universe, for example, light depends on darkness and darkness on light. We could not know what light is without having darkness to compare with light.

Curiosity wonders, "What am I?" Attention narrows, imagination posits, and assumption concludes: "I am X." Each theory is the basis of an entire universe. Curiosity is never satisfied through this search because each theory is inevitably incomplete, but like a child it plays on in its excitement. Through this play of self-definition, countless universes bubble out into what is called the multiverse. Remember, all of these universes represent potentiality, and because there is no time from the holistic perspective of Isness, all possibilities are in the very same moment, yet the clouded mind frames these potentialities in a moment-by-moment progression in order to grasp them, which is the effect of time. Thus time both is and is not dependent upon perspective, which is to say within the clouded mind time is real, but outside it time is not.

Some core commonalities exist among all universes, namely the desire to define the self, as well as the instability and disharmony that this desire causes. Another commonality is the unconscious desire to find balance within an inherently imbalanced system. These two primary desires stimulate a great game of musical chairs throughout the multiverse, where everything is vying for a permanent, safe position but never able to find one through the effort because all theories of self are inherently untrue, and, therefore, unstable.

Because the multiverse is a projection of the desire for self-definition, which is an illusion, the multiverse itself is not ultimately true. We could look at the multiverse as the pearl that forms around a single grain of sand which represents the sense of otherness. The physics of any particular universe are determined by the nature of that grain of sand — the specific theory of self that the clouded mind collapsed upon.

Looking at the ongoing process of the clouded mind, "What am I?" does not yet represent as a universe, although it does stimulate speculation. When speculation creates a premis to answer the question, "What am I?" that premis of self necessarily projects a sense of other to contrast with the premis of self. As soon as an answer to the question "What am I?" is formed, a mind-bubble of manifestation, a universe, expands in order to fully explore that conclusion. From elementary particles, to subatomic particles, to atoms, to molecules, to structures such as stars, planets, galaxies, and solar systems — and ultimately to organisms – the premis of self is explored to get as many perspectives on the premis as possible. At the moment the bubble begins to expand, time is present, and things begin to appear in relativistic, linear cause-and-effect relationships — i.e., experience.

Surrounding our own physical universe are many varieties of universes that have aspects of our universe, as well as some that are so vastly different as to be inconceivable to us. Many of the otherworldly experiences that people have had under powerful hallucinogens are a result of opening psychic doorways into other universes and dimensions in the multiverse. But all of these universes are still projections of self, otherness, and assumption, so we should be just as careful about following the wisdom of individuals from these other universes as we are about following the wisdom of people in our universe.

The nature of the mind is found in the attempt to define the self. But because there is no actual self or form to define, assumption willfully projects form through imagination. The form must always exist in opposition because we need the illusion of other to sustain the illusion of self. For example, strength can be understood only in contrast to weakness. Therefore, everything that stems from otherness is perceived through contrasting opposites: masculine versus feminine, high versus low, near versus far, good versus evil, etc. Because definition and opposition are the origins of the clouded mind, definition and opposition are what a clouded mind naturally does. It's all that a clouded mind can do. It has no choice. It defines, and it contrasts.

In actuality, there is only the timeless moment of *being*, and there truly is no self to identify; so, for example, whatever is projected is inherently unstable. And what is unstable suffers change and decay, which causes the sense of time in the multiverse. Therefore, all that is bound in the multiverse must break down and/or change. Disharmony is the inevitable outcome of the conclusions of mind, as is the effect of becoming.

Yet through and beyond the cloud of mind exists Isness, and, therefore, disharmony is not the only possibility. There is always the chance for clarity when the mind is not fed through ignorance and speculation. What would this state look like? It's the unconditioned acceptance of being, without any further attempt to define the self while lovingly observing the totality with authority.

This perspective relaxes into and enjoys *being* without trying to define itself. Isness observes and accepts formless nonduality, and, therefore, it's not divided or bound in any way. Buddhism indicates it as the Eternal Buddha. The New Testament calls it the Holy Father. Taoism indicates it as the Tao. There may be many terms that indicate the same thing. But no matter the term, rightly understood, it's not really a name but just an indication or hint.

The possibility of unconditioned consciousness does not name, describe, or define itself so long as it's unconditioned. The possibility that names or describes itself is conditioned and bound in the multiverse. Remember, any attempt to define the self creates a mental bubble, which is disharmony, change, decay, and time — the multiverse.

Consider that a developing human embryo goes from undifferentiated being to greater and greater differentiation. A newborn baby doesn't know the difference between its body and the surrounding environment. It has to develop a sense of self and other to navigate the environment that surrounds its body. And as the sensory definitions refine, the baby gains greater function within the universe. But in the process of self-development, the individual forgets the undifferentiated awareness of being. It forgets Soul, and therefore suffers. Fortunately, it is possible to unbind awareness from the self and regain conscious connection to Soul, but one must first begin to embrace nondefining, unconditioned acceptance of being.

The wonderful thing about the possibility of nondefining, unconditioned acceptance of being is that it observes the projecting process without judgment, for it understands that the multiverse is purely the natural outcome of defining the self; it's not a mistake, it's a possibility. Consciousness and mind are potential perspectives: the former, all inclusive; the latter, exclusive, and existing within the smallest, most fundamental building blocks, elementary particles, as well as the largest celestial objects of the multiverse, and even within you.

~Chapter 11~
Frequencies of Mind and Consciousness

When a superior man hears of the Tao,
he immediately begins to embody it.
When an average man hears of the Tao,
he half believes it, half doubts it.
When a foolish man hears of the Tao,
he laughs out loud.
If he didn't laugh,
it wouldn't be the Tao.

— *Tao Te Ching*

Just as ignorance and speculation create mental bubbles that are universes, so does the individual within the multiverse create mental bubbles by way of defining the self, and with each bubble created, the individual's conscious awareness is further veiled, making it more and more challenging to maintain the holistic perspective of consciousness. Each mental bubble we have, such as "I am a doctor" or "I am smart," becomes an identification that must feed in order to survive. Each time we associate ourselves with or react to disharmony, we are feeding an identification with Soul energy.

These identifications swarm, parasitizing Soul energy. This swarm of chaotic disharmony creates a veil which blocks the individual from realizing Isness at the very core. Because the individual is identified with these definitions and limitations, the very sense of self is on the line whenever we illuminate the phenomenon. Because of the tendency for identifications to fight back and to protect themselves, the reader may experience difficulties when reading this book as the light of consciousness begins to shine through those identifications that do not want to be seen.

If we look at this resistance as an opportunity to see behind the curtain of our own consciousness, then what resistance allows us is an incredible opportunity, depending on our attitude toward it. It's wise, when resistance comes up, to patiently observe it and let the dust settle within before reading on. Otherwise, we will be moving through a cloud of dust that will reduce visibility. Because we are going to be learning to observe the mind, it will be helpful to have a common understanding of typical mental activities, such as thought, imagination, memory, emotion, and the senses, with which to work. Minus a common language to work with, there is too much room for misunderstanding. So let's use the Merriam-Webster Online Dictionary to draw our definitions.

Thought: an idea, plan, opinion, picture, etc., that is formed in your mind: something that you think of.

Imagination: the ability to imagine things that are not real: the ability to form a picture in your mind of something that you have not seen or experienced.

Memory: the power or process of remembering what has been learned.

Emotion: a strong feeling (such as love, anger, joy, hate, or fear); feelings.

Senses: the five natural powers (touch, taste, smell, sight, and hearing) through which you receive information about the world around you.

Are we always thinking? Almost always, yes, but this does not have to be the case, which we will get into shortly. With regard to thinking, consider driving down the road in a car. You see all the other cars on the road in front of you, and you are able to drive well without thinking about it, assuming you are a competent driver. You'd recognize the brands of cars around you without having a labeling process occur in your mind like, "Ford," "Toyota," "Chevy," etc. If you are a skilled driver, there might be no particular noise in your head actively making such identifications as you are driving, right? Instead, you know by association. You see a Ford and you know it's a Ford. You see this book, and you know what it is without mentally saying to yourself, "This is a book." To say to yourself, "This is a book" is a thought.When we are competent at something such as driving, we are not thinking about driving. Instead we are often thinking about other things as the mind meanders to this topic or that, or we might be trying to solve a problem that we are having at work, for example. Constant thinking does not have to be the case, though, which we will get to in a bit.

Speculating is thinking, and thinking leads to thought. For example, "I wonder what kind of animal it was that just crossed the road in front of me? It was too big to be a cat. The movement was not really like a dog's. It had stripes on its bushy tail. It must have been a raccoon." This is thinking that led to the conclusion in the thought, "I saw a raccoon."

How do senses reinforce the mind? If you pay attention to how you use your senses, you will notice that you perceive something that stimulates an associated meaning within you. For example, you are driving along and you see a raccoon cross the road, and before you know it your mind has gone into a memory of when you were a boy and your father took you raccoon hunting. The next thing you know, your mind leaps into imagination as you think about what that meat might have tasted like if you had killed one and had to eat it. You might have an emotional response to the thought of eating a raccoon. Next, you notice that you are little hungry, so you think about what you might have for lunch. You decide on a fast food drive-through, then you remember that the last time you ate in the car, you spilled soda on the crotch of your pants and then were too embarrassed to go to work, so you had to go home and change pants, which made you late. Your face actually reddens at the memory of it as you feel the emotion of embarrassment in your body.

Just like thinking, imagination and memory cause mental noise, all of which can be stimulated by associated meanings connected to what your senses pick up in your environment. Emotion may pop up here and there throughout the process. Can you imagine what it would be like to drive down the road in a totally relaxed, yet alert silence, feeling as if you were vastly and lovingly connected to everything? This is a taste of the consciousness of which I speak. Of course, you may just be imagining it, which is not consciousness, but you get the idea – again not consciousness.

For most people, thoughts, imagination, memories, and emotions are almost constantly moving around in the mind, stimulated by associations the senses trigger, and the only times of respite are when the moment is so intense and exhilarating that there is no time for thought, such as when we are bungee jumping or playing a fast-paced competitive game. In such a moment, there isn't enough time for the movement of thought, or if there were, thinking would cause us to lose if the opponent were truly competent. At such an intense moment, there is heightened mental silence. Unfortunately, there is also a lot of focused intention, which tires us and eventually leads into dullness. By far the most common cause of mental silence is when we are too tired or dulled from poor health to have much mental activity. This is not a healthy thing.

So how do we step out of the mind and into consciousness? We can use the idea of frequencies as a good model to explain the differences between mind and consciousness. When the mind is active, I perceive energy fields resonating strongly in proximity to the body, which I suspect to some degree constitute the magnetic field that is sometimes referred to as the aura. The energy of this aura comes from biological processes of the body and mind.

During deep states of meditation, you may feel a clear, harmonious field radiating out much further than does the aura. Thus for instructional purposes we will say that the mind resonates at lower frequencies than consciousness. An easy way to conceptualize these fields for communication purposes is to imagine them radiating like the electromagnetic spectrum. We could break up the different frequencies into classes or bands similar to the bands of color in the rainbow. Let's take a look at the frequencies of mind as if they exist along the electromagnetic spectrum, which is commonly divided into seven classes of waves.

Electromagnetic Spectrum Classes:
1 - Radio
2 - Microwave
3 - Infrared
4 - Visible
5 - Ultraviolet

6 - X-ray
7 - Gamma ray
Mental Spectrum Classes:
8 - Emotion, Feelings, Will
9 - Thought, Imagination, Memory

Besides the mental classes, there are higher frequency classes that are of consciousness. These spectrums are the harmonious fields that lead to resolution of the self when activated by intention. I have given several associated descriptions that resonate with each frequency class, but these are not the only descriptions that we could use.

Harmonious Frequency Classes:
10 - Curiosity, Relaxation, Innocence
11 - Observation, Sharing, Compassion
12 - Silence, Acceptance, Appreciation
13+ - Unconditioned Love

The use of the mind is always a double-edged sword. Although using the mind can serve practical purposes within the multiverse, each time that we use it an agitation occurs which is the feeding of identifications. For this reason, I indicate the frequencies of mind as being disharmonious. This is not a judgment against the mind, but an observation of the price we pay for using it.

As I run through various scenarios of mind and consciousness, I will use parentheses to indicate the frequencies being tuned to. For example, fear would be followed by (8) and would be written "fear(8)" in the text. As a sentence, it might appear this way: "Fear(8) is in the frequency of emotion(8), so it carries disharmony(8-9)." I recommend the reader observe their own mind while reading and frequently refer to the spectrums to note the frequencies being tuned to.

Through the process of intentional unfoldment, we tune to consciousness(11+), the transformative frequencies that purify and remove divisions.

Curiosity(10) and innocence(10), are natural portals to consciousness(11+). When we begin to question(10) all assumptions about the self(8-9), we then have the opening through which resolution can begin to occur. Curiosity is not to be confused with thinking(9) for they are distinct fields. Curiosity leaves the door open for inspirience and insight, whereas thinking is biased(9) by one's paradigm(9). Thinking is entirely of the self, whereas questioning innocently is an open portal to consciousness(11+) as long as it does not turn to speculation(9). This is why I strongly encourage my students to be playfully curious. Adults have such difficulty with curiosity, but for young children curiosity is natural because innocence is not yet blocked by knowledge(9) or ignorance(8).

We should not confuse innocence(10) with ignorance(8). Innocence is open, whereas ignorance is closed. Look closely at the word "ignor-ance" to get a sense of how I am using it. To ignore is a willful(8) act, and that is why ignorance is disharmonious(8-9). Innocence, on the other hand, is open and, therefore, harmonious(10+). Consider that innocence is defined as being blameless and as lacking the knowledge(9) of right and wrong. It's not willful because it's open.

Consider *Genesis:* "And out of the ground the Lord God made every tree grow that is pleasant to the sight and good for food. The tree of life was also in the midst of the garden, and the tree of the knowledge of good and evil." If we were to say that the tree of the knowledge of good and evil represents self-consciousness(8-9), then the tree of life represents Christ-consciousness. The allegory continues with a warning that Adam and Eve may eat freely of all trees in the garden except the tree of the knowledge of good and evil, which is located at the center of the garden. Should they eat of the tree of the knowledge of good and evil, they are warned that they will surely die.

Adam and Eve ultimately ignore the warning and eat the forbidden fruit in hopes of gaining the power of God. From this allegory, we can see that the desire(8) of knowledge(9) for the sake of selfish power causes great disharmony(8-9). Then there is the concept that knowledge brings about a sense of opposing contrasts(otherness), which are represented as good and evil, judgments of the self-conscious mind(8-9). Could this be a warning that using the mind thus births disharmony?

After eating of the fruit of this tree, Adam and Eve know that they are naked, and so they sew fig leaves together to cover their shame. Before eating the forbidden fruit, Adam and Eve are similar to small children or animals in that they are not self-conscious. Eating of that tree births self-consciousness(8-9), which covers over innocence(10).

Later, when they hear the sound of God walking in the garden, Adam and Eve hide themselves among the trees of the garden in fear because they are naked. When God questions them, Adam justifies himself by indirectly blaming God, saying that Eve, whom God made for him, persuaded him to eat the fruit. When God questions Eve, she blames the serpent for deceiving her. Clearly, we can see fear, blame, and justification expressing for the first time through Adam and Eve. All three of these energies are corrupt children of self-consciousness.

The allegory continues with the birth of enmity between humans and serpents, with the beginnings of suffering through pain, and the need to toil for food. Humankind now begins to experience death.

God then drives Adam and Eve out of the garden, and he places cherubim east of the garden of Eden, and a flaming sword which turned every way, to guard the way to the tree of life. Cherubim are angels, like heavenly signposts that beckon us to the gate. The flaming sword totally blocks all inappropriate access into the garden to eat of the tree of life, Christ-consciousness. Because the flaming sword blocks access in every direction, nothing can enter, which is to say, *no thing* can enter. Only when totally free of self content can we reenter the garden to eat of the tree of life and thereby end suffering(8-9).

At first glance, the beginnings of self-consciousness would appear to be a mistake, but it is not. After the development of self-consciousness, quite naturally, self content accumulates via emotions of fear and shame and subsequent thoughts of self-definition, such as "I am afraid" and "I am naked and ashamed." Fundamentally, we are speaking of a sense of vulnerability.

At some point, the individual becomes self-aware to the point of noticing that self content is a millstone around the neck. Then the individual begins to question the very sense of self and the sense of separation, at which time self content can be observed and resolved through the frequencies of consciousness (11+). These harmonious frequencies allow for resolution of this disharmonious content through removing all feeling-level associations as well as intellectual definitions of the self. As self content resolves, one becomes more harmonious and naturally gravitates ever closer to the gates of Eden. Ego caused Adam and Eve's disharmony(8-9), and, therefore, innocence(10) is the first step to reentering Eden.

The desire(8) for knowledge(9), which is erroneously perceived as power, smothers innocence(10) and then bars reentry into Eden. Therefore, we must revitalize innocence, but in order to do so we must begin to see through the illusion of the self(8-9), and for that we must also revitalize curiosity(10). Curiosity through innocence is what begins the process of resolving the self. Consider these sayings attributed to Jesus: "Truly I tell you, unless you change and become like little children, you will never enter the kingdom of Heaven," and "Truly I tell you, anyone who will not receive the kingdom of God like a little child will never enter it."

There is an innocence(10) to young children that allows for curiosity(10). The knowledge(9) of "wise" elders jades(8) and biases(9) all perspective, thereby closing the door of innocence and curiosity. This is why adults typically lack curiosity, and this is a true blockage because the natural doorway to consciousness(11+) is innocent curiosity.

We must be careful with curiosity, though, because curiosity can easily be corrupted by ego-based motivations. Many criminals are very curious, but that curiosity is directed toward personal gain, not toward unfoldment. In such a case, curiosity becomes the boot that kicks one out of the garden. Motivation is essential to the unfoldment process, which is why curiosity through innocence is an essential distinction.

So innocent(10) curiosity(10) assists in tuning to conscious(11+) frequencies that begin the process of resolving identifications (8-9). The higher the frequency of harmony, the more transformative is the field. The potential for these harmonious frequencies is always there, but this potential is actualized only when activated by intent. Human beings, unlike animals, have the innate capacity to work with these frequencies by mere intent as we unfold precisely because we are self-conscious. The frequencies of consciousness automatically represent our intent so long as our intent is not blocked by identifications(8-9), a dark band that veils the light within.

Curiosity used rightly is a vital tool in the process of unfoldment, but it's not the only tool. There is also meditation, which greatly speeds the process. Using meditation, we tune to observation(11), and then, little by little, as disharmony(8-9) sloughs off, we become able to tune to higher frequencies without using willpower(8). Unconditioned love(13+) is what we are ultimately moving toward, but having it as an idea(9) or philosophy(9) is not the same thing as actually tuning in to that frequency because the thought(9) of unconditioned love is still exercising the mind(8-9), which incorporates disharmonious frequencies.

Many individuals I have met who embrace the philosophy(9) of unconditioned love(13+) are actually emitting the frequencies of thought(9) and emotion(8). They are in love(8) with the idea(9) of love, which is not unconditioned love. There is a frequency of love in the class of emotion, but it's a personal love(8), which, albeit high in the frequency of emotion, is not unconditioned(11+). Personal love and unconditioned love are not to be confused.

In order to prime students and guide them up to the higher frequencies without going into willfulness(8) or stimulating the thought(9) of love(8) or the emotion(8) of love, which are of the self(8-9), we practice the Observation Meditation, which I detail in the next chapter. The Observation Meditation quickly tunes us to the frequency of the 11th class of the conscious(11+) spectrum, where disharmony can be addressed productively.

It sounds to me as if you are suggesting that thinking is wrong. That I should be thoughtless. Wouldn't that make me a very foolish person?

It is very interesting how we call foolish people thoughtless. The truth is that foolish people are not thoughtless. In fact, they may have a lot of thoughts, but those thoughts may not be sharp or skillful. Sometimes a foolish person may indeed not have many thoughts, but this is because they are tuned to a frequency below thought, which creates the effect of dullness. If you were to reflect on your thinking and thoughts over a normal week, what percentage of your thinking and thoughts, do you think, are necessary?

I see where you're going with this. You are saying I do a lot of unnecessary thinking, which is true. But I do a lot of necessary thinking as well, especially for my job.

Be aware that the structures of our society are of mind, which means our economic system, governments, politics, businesses, education system, buildings, jobs, relationships — all structure, really, is designed through mind, which means that working in them tends to pull us into mind if we are not careful. Once the majority of people are tuned to consciousness, the structures of society will begin to change quite dramatically, and then working in those structures will require being tuned to consciousness, which at least means much less thinking.

Practically speaking, in our current society, we will begin tuning to consciousness and spend less energy in mind. We will think only when we have to, and tune to consciousness when we don't have to. You may find that a lot of what you currently believe to be necessary thinking becomes less and less necessary as you tune more to consciousness.

~Chapter 12~
Observation Meditation

Words of warning before one embarks on this type of meditation: The Observation Meditation, although pleasurable and inspiring, will bring up unconscious darkness to be observed and resolved, sometimes during the meditation but usually afterward. The things that come up may be that which we have not wanted to see. The process of unfoldment is for those who are tired of deceiving themselves and who are willing to slough through the seemingly endless amounts of muck in order to reach the shores of enlightenment.

This meditation was inspired by the Amazon vision and ultimately realized through the combined training of both martial and therapy arts during my time in Japan. Through training in the martial arts, I gained appreciation for the power of fluid stability under pressure. A good instructor gradually exposes us to increasing levels of pressure and difficulty until we are able to handle real attacks with grace. In much the same way, we want to find fluid stability in our meditation so that grace can shine through the disharmony of everyday life. If we are not being challenged, then we are probably not making much progress.

The Observation Meditation is a fundamental and highly refined tool that I use to guide individuals through the unfoldment process. As you may not have personal access to meditation coaching, we will start with a sedentary meditation and work on what we can without a coach. Although we will start out seated, we will quickly progress into more activity and greater challenge. It will feel like a baby learning to see, then crawl, then walk, run, and so on.

We will initially use the senses in an unconditioned way to springboard into a more pure meditation. I use this form of meditation because it does not incorporate any religious symbolism, and all that is necessary for its practice is readily available to you through your physical body. Its greatest value is in its natural simplicity. For anyone who lacks in any of the physical senses, just skip them and work with what you have. As your system will have compensated for any missing senses, you should still reach the same energetic place as anyone with full access to all their senses. Also, remember that we will quickly progress beyond the senses, as we do not want to have any crutches.

Set a timer to 30 minutes for your first session and add a few minutes to each session thereafter. The more time that we grant to this meditation, the more stability we will achieve. Find a comfortable place to sit, but do not rest your back against anything unless you must do so for such circumstances as injury or pain.

Sit comfortably on the floor or in a chair to begin, gaze straight ahead, and extend your arms out to your sides (palms forward) so that they are just outside your visual field. Bend your wrists so that your palms are facing the sides of your face and wiggle your fingers. Slowly bring your arms forward until you can just barely see the tips of your wiggling fingers while gazing straight ahead. This is the horizontal range of your visual field. Generally it will be nearly 180 degrees for most people.

Next, move one hand down, below your abdomen, and one hand up, high above your head, until they are outside your visual field. Wiggling your fingers, slowly move them forward until you can find the vertical range of your visual field. Once you are aware of the vertical limits of the field, move your hands circularly to find the entire outer edge of the visual field.

This is the field that your eyes pick up at all times but that your mind selectively and unconsciously edits to the point where more often than not you perceive only a small portion of what comes into the field. An example of this selective awareness is what happens when we read. As we read we are almost entirely unaware of what occurs outside the page unless we try to be aware of what's happening around us as readers.

Once familiar and comfortable with the total visual field, rest your arms, and we'll move on to the next step in the meditation, sound. Pay attention to the total auditory field. Allow yourself to become unconditionally aware of all sounds around you. Just allow all sound to enter the body unfettered, and do not allow your attention to latch onto individual sounds.

Relax into unconditioned awareness of both the visual and auditory fields for several minutes to become accustomed to them in their unconditioned state. We want to be as relaxed as possible in this process, but at the same time not allow the physical body to be too slack, as that may cause drowsiness and lead to inattentiveness or sleep. Continue with your attention on the visual and auditory fields for several minutes before moving on to the next step.

Next, become aware of the entire surface area of the body. Pay attention to the feeling of the clothing and air touching your skin, the feeling of gravity pulling on the body, the floor beneath you, etc. Do not allow your attention to focus on any particular point on or in the body. If you have aches and pains, allow the attention to spread out and not condense at these points. Remain aware of the body in this way for several minutes before moving on to the next step.

Next, become aware of the olfactory sense, the sense of smell. You may notice the smells in the room, the smell of your own body and the smell of the food that you have eaten earlier in the day. Do not allow yourself to get caught up in the process of labeling individual smells, however. Just smell purely and unconditionally without labeling anything.

In warmer temperatures, smells are easier to detect than in cold environs. Also, when the nostrils are moist, they will pick up smells better than when dry. So, do not be concerned if, on some days, you are able to notice smells better than on other days. Moreover, some people have a much better sense of smell than others. Do not be concerned with how much you can smell, but instead pay attention to the sense itself and the feeling inside the nostrils as the air moves through them. Again, relax into this process and maintain unconditioned awareness of all previous senses.

Finally, we move on to the sense of taste and the feeling within the mouth. You will probably be able to taste some or many of the things that you have eaten throughout the day, but in the event that you do not, have no concern. Just relax into the sense of taste and the feeling within the mouth. Give yourself a few minutes to acclimate to the sense of taste while remaining unconditionally aware of all other senses.

At this stage of the meditation, our awareness is extended much more than it would typically be. Although the extent of our awareness is important, it's not the only thing we are looking for here. The natural habit for most people new to this form of meditation is to rely on eyesight for most of their awareness, creating an egg-shaped field of awareness. Because modern humans have the tendency to be visually focused, attention is almost entirely to the front, which causes physiological imbalance and stress.

What we are working toward is a perfect, spherical awareness that extends equally in every direction from the center of the body. The way to tune to this sphericality is to start giving some attention to all directions through feeling, but do not be too willful; instead, relax into it. Gradually our addiction to the visual sense will break, and, little by little, we will be more functionally attentive to the total space around us.

Once relaxed and fully into the meditation, begin moving a little while maintaining unconditioned awareness. You might move an arm or a leg, for example, or look around. From my experience coaching people, their energy fields tend to collapse while moving in the early stages until they acclimate and gain more stability in the process. This indicates the unconscious use of the mind. It's good to challenge oneself little by little, moving arms and legs, getting up and sitting down, etc.

Start out using the senses as I have instructed, but quickly wean yourself of this technique. Within a few meditation sessions, you should no longer need to use your arms to find the visual field; nor will you need to go through the path of your senses, but instead you will simply be attentive to and feel the total space around you.

There will be days on which the meditation practice seems flat and other days on which it's truly inspiring. Do not be concerned at all with outcomes, as this perspective is egoic. Just make time to meditate and allow each session to be unique. Sometimes we may be highly distracted and have the strong temptation to quit, feeling it's a waste of time. The last thing we should do in this case is quit. Instead lightly and gently look into what it is that is distracting you. When you see that something within does not want you meditating, then you realize that the worst thing you could do is to quit. Stay the course even if that means just sitting there for the allotted time.

When we consider any noteworthy accomplishment in the world, the person or persons who achieved it were unfailingly persistent. I once enjoyed a conversation with a retired Navy SEAL, who told me that the SEAL selection process is very simple. They put the potential recruits through Hell and see who gives up. If the individual gets through the tests, even if they do not look spectacular, then they are accepted into SEAL training. But the vast majority of people quit.

The quitter is an identification that people feed during the small activities of their lives. They quit at things that they consider insignificant first, and in this way they start feeding the quitter. With each quitting experience the quitter gets stronger and stronger, and pretty soon its voice is overwhelming. "It's boring. It takes too long. It's too much work. It's too troublesome. It hurts. I can't. It's impossible. Someone let me out of this, please." These are some of its seductive utterances.

If we have fed the quitter, then we can start to resolve it through meditation and through the smaller activities of our lives. Little by little, we will face challenges without quitting. With regard to unfoldment, it's not necessary to be a tremendous athlete or to be incredibly academic, but it's exceedingly important to be persistent over the long term, as this process can take years or lifetimes, depending on the individual and the specific path we are walking. In any case, in the mind there must never be a finish line. Sometimes people ask me when I will stop practicing martial arts. To me this question is like asking when I will quit breathing. There is no end as far as my intention is concerned. Just keep moving forward.

There is a lot more to be understood in this process than I have been able to explain in this section, much of which we will realize through continued meditation practice. I cannot state enough how important the Observation Meditation is. Remember to keep it simple and keep your eyes open. Do not allow into this process any crutches, such as the use of spiritual symbols, spiritual items, or anything else; keep it pure. We are already born with all we need to unfold, and the more crutches we use, the less applicable the meditation will be to our daily lives. We are now at a point in the consciousness of this planet when spirituality needs to be more than just a hobby, sideshow, or weekend activity; instead, it needs to be lived. Have faith in your unfoldment process, and abandon all that is nonessential.

Consistency is the key to this meditation. The more we practice the easier it is to remain tuned to consciousness. We will also find, with consistent practice, that the things which used to easily knock us out of consciousness no longer have much impact on us. Immerse yourself whenever you can, but remember that even a moment here or a second there is greatly beneficial. It would be much better to meditate even for a few seconds than to not meditate at all. Set a meditation regimen that you know you will actually do every day. All that we need to do is get some momentum going with regard to meditation.

Ultimately we want to develop a life-pattern that supports meditation over the long-run. As it gets easier and easier to remain in the frequencies of consciousness, we will have time to incorporate it into our life and make necessary structural changes that support the unfoldment process. Many of our blockages are structural, which is to say the blockages are found in our life-patterns. We want this process to become a part of our daily life so that meditation and life are one and the same. There simply is no substitute for daily meditation in this regard.

Deconditioning Meditation

There are many types of meditations in the world, each with unique features and differing aims. Some of these methods are very good for relaxation, for religious practice, or for healing the body. Some of these meditations make use of rituals, symbols, sound devices, music, or chanting. While almost any meditation is highly beneficial, some methods are more applicable to unfoldment through daily life than others. Because a human being's life experience is nothing like the conditions of these meditations, I have found that they do not translate well into our daily lives, which are active and chaotic by comparison to the meditation methods being practiced. The specific conditions of these meditations have become obstacles to functional silence in daily life, and since it's through our daily life that unfoldment occurs, conditioned meditation is not very applicable.

I have also found that the more austere forms of meditation are in general not very beneficial to initiates in daily life because the individual is highly unstable, thanks to emotion, thought, and sensation. As such, the individual's amount of mental chatter and unconscious reactivity is tremendous. Because of the magnitude and intensity of unconscious disharmony, it's easy to be distracted, or bored, or disturbed, or go into willfulness. The result is that many who are eager for unfoldment find these types of meditations to be boring, impractical, and/or prohibitively difficult, which is why so few individuals are able to stick with the process over the long term.

Within a few months of Observation Meditation practice — which is a dynamic, unconditioned method, one's awareness would be more spherical and would extend farther out in daily life, indicative of a less conditioned self. I have seen no other form of meditation that produces such rapid, stable results. The reason for the rapid progress through the Observation Meditation is that it's designed to embrace what would normally disturb others. By expanding awareness, it naturally provides more conscious and physical stability. I quickly have students up and moving to challenge their stability and to find applicable expansion for daily life.

First, they practice listening and speaking until they develop enough stability to maintain expansive awareness. One would think that listening and talking during meditation would be simple, but it's surprisingly difficult for newcomers and even those who have practiced sedentary meditations for years. Once they gain some stability with conversation, they then practice standing and walking without collapsing. Continuing with this expansion into daily activities, this process eventually enables the individual to fully function under high pressure and not collapse back into mind. Because this form of meditation is so dynamic, people find it to be extremely soothing yet also challenging and inspiring.

Through the Observation Meditation, people are able to gain more stability and functionality while remaining rooted in a more loving and connected way through their actual lives. Little by little, through observation, individuals root their lives in consciousness. Many students who are somewhat new to the process ask me what it feels like to be tuned in this way, and the best way I can describe it is as a constant, clear, loving, vastness. A person bound in the spectrums of emotion, thought, and the conditioned senses would feel finite, small, stagnant, and turbulent.

Sometimes you might wonder whether your meditation sessions are productive. If you've made the time and gone through the process, it was productive. Making the time and space for the meditation process is really the key, especially early in the effort. If we are too busy to set aside much time, then do it while on break, on the toilet, or while walking. Even a minute here or a minute there is good. Meditate while driving, while on trains, and in any spare moment. Just keep at it and, eventually, it's constant. Doing so, I was able to maintain higher frequencies through all activities of my life and find sublime silence. It's no longer meditation; it's life.

Initially we will be using all of our senses to go into meditation, which will require a lot of intent, so we will look like zombies. This is natural because we are completely retuning our awareness away from the conditioning of the self toward unconditionality. Once we retune fully through our daily life, we will always have stability through Isness, and there will be no need for us to meditate to be in harmony.

Remember that the Observation Meditation as I have described it is a powerful step in the process of spiritual unfoldment, so no matter how far along the path we go, the fundamentals that we find through this method will serve to illuminate the path. Keep it simple, and allow it to purify your life.

You have said using the senses reinforces the mind, yet you are using senses in your introductory meditation. Why is that?

When we use some senses to the exclusion of the other senses, which is what people habitually do, it leads us back into the mind. But when the senses all work together in an unconditioned fashion, there is a harmonic effect that tunes us to the 11th frequency class, which is harmonious.

I am a very low-energy person. It's very difficult for me to remain alert and even sit up straight because I just feel dull all the time. How do I meditate if I don't have energy?

I also found this to be a real challenge on days of dullness. I chose not to fight the dullness but instead to flow with it. Lie down on your back and bend your knees so that the bottoms of your feet are flat on the floor to keep the lower back from arching too much. Put your arms out to your sides on the floor, bending them at the elbow 90 degrees while keeping your lightly clenched fists up in the air. The goal is to keep the knees and hands up through the meditation process while being as relaxed as possible. If you start to doze off, then the knees and hands will begin to fall and that is likely to awaken you enough to correct the posture and remain in the meditation.

Often I found I would enter a kind of twilight state just between being asleep and being awake, but still able to observe. That's a fine meditation that I came out of clear and refreshed. If you lose circulation to your hands, put them down for a time until the blood flows back and rejuvenates them, then put them back up. If you find that keeping your knees up is enough to keep you alert, then you can just use your legs and relax your arms. Play with it to find what works for you.

For some people, lying on the back is uncomfortable, so we can modify this process if we look at the principles. Find a position that is comfortable and create a light focal point with the body to stimulate alertness. For example, if lying on our right side, we could place our left hand on our left hip with the elbow bent and pointed at the ceiling. The key in this example is to keep the elbow pointed at the ceiling. When you become more proficient, you can sit with tension in your outstretched fingers preventing the fingertips from touching your lap. All of these methods serve to keep just enough attention to be successful but not so much that it becomes uncomfortable or willful.

If this tension method does not work, take a cold bath or shower just before meditating, and consider getting a little more sleep if you are sleep deprived. If that still does not help, see your health practitioner as there may be some health issues that need addressing. We do not want to build an unconscious association with sleep during this process because once that association begins then meditations will put you to sleep consistently, which is counterproductive.

~Chapter 13~
Potential Pitfalls

In pursuit of knowledge, every day something is added.
In the practice of the Tao, every day something is dropped.
Less and less do you need to force things,
until finally you arrive at non-action.
When nothing is done, nothing is left undone.

— *Tao Te Ching*

As I have stated, the process of unfoldment is a revelation of what is and always has been, therefore we must be very careful about adding to this process. Techniques, modalities, skills, etc., are all potentially dangerous distractions taking us away from unfoldment as we become dependent upon these things. What we are looking for in this process is to discover the core and the fundamental, so we strip away all that is unnecessary as we go.

All techniques and tools that I teach are only temporary and will soon be discarded as the individual discovers the principles behind the techniques. Therefore, although we do respect the tools and techniques so far as they assist us to move beyond them, we do not allow ourselves to become reliant upon them. The self will most certainly do its best to turn each and every thing into a crutch, so we must be "careful as a warrior in enemy territory" as Lao-Tzu puts it.

Eventually, we will find that nothing other than unconditioned love is necessary, and that will be the natural effect of your very being, not something that you do. Until then, we do what we can to strip away and find the purity within, while tuning to the frequencies of consciousness as often as possible.

Techniques and Comfort Zones

Many people will have a technique or visualization that makes it seem easier to meditate, but such things invariably lead to imbalance and become crutches upon which dependence quickly develops. Remember, we are looking to strip away all nonessentials so that we have stability in our high-speed, high-pressure lives.

Keep it simple and pure even if it seems a little more difficult initially that way. You will come to appreciate this advice in short order. Also, be careful not to meditate in the same comfortable place and position. Little by little, expose yourself to potential distractions and new locations while also sitting in different positions, facing in different directions. At my first training center, which was in town, we had a dance studio just above our space. The building was more than 100 years old, and there was no insulation between their floor and our ceiling, so effectively their hardwood floor and our false ceiling made a giant speaker. When they danced, it sounded like a buffalo ballet. Throw in the music, and you have a herd of disco-dancing water buffalo.

Initially there was the thought that it would be a bad place to meditate, but I challenged that assumption and had my beginning students meditate through the racket. What they found was they were distracted only if they held a negative attitude toward the music. If we just allow for the "distraction" it quickly ceases to have any power over us. If we practice accepting attitudes in our lives we will find that a lot of "distractions" lose power over us.

Willfulness

Modern people around the world hail willfulness as being a virtue since all that we do in modern culture is based on force. But willfulness is firmly in the frequency of disharmony, so it's not an effective vehicle for tuning to harmony. Pay attention to what happens in your mind when experiencing willfulness. Everything closes in to exclusion as the mind focuses on what it's going to forcefully accomplish. At this moment there is strength in only one direction and weakness in every other direction. This is not the way of consciousness; it's of the mind. The power of consciousness is distributed equally in all directions because it's unconditioned and unbiased.

Be aware of willfulness as it arises in the meditation process, and instead of feeding willfulness, try relaxing into the process. We set a goal of using no more than 10 percent of our attention to do anything in particular. The more time given to this process, the less effort will be required to do it. Initially, you may look like a zombie, but as you acclimate and incorporate it into your daily life, it will be more and more natural and, of course, beneficial.

How can we accomplish anything without willpower? Lao-Tzu gives us a hint: "Do you have the patience to wait until your mud settles and the water is clear? Can you remain unmoving until the right action arises by itself?" Instead of using force and willfulness to accomplish, we need to find another avenue, which is consciousness. There will come a point at which the body will just accomplish things on its own. When this first happens it will be quite astounding, but eventually it will feel normal. No matter how often it happens, it will always be inspiring because it does not come from the mind.

Until it begins to occur, practice the 10 percent rule that we use during meditation. The rule goes this way: Never use more than 10 percent of your focus on any particular thing; instead, keep awareness spread out evenly. In this manner we are able to accomplish without feeding willfulness and force. Keep some awareness spread out and open to the environment within and around the body. This is sure to be difficult at first, especially during very challenging tasks, but eventually we are able to do things in this way, which ultimately leads into the body moving on its own to accomplish tasks.

Artifacts

In meditation, especially in the early stages, one may experience what I call artifacts. Artifacts are strange visual phenomena that sometimes show up during meditation. The frequencies of consciousness will initially be beyond the brain's ability to work with, which will create odd effects such as the appearance of a funny haze over the floor. The walls or ceilings may appear to be undulating. The room may appear to brighten and darken repeatedly, or suddenly the whole visual field may collapse entirely and leave you in total darkness, even though your eyes are open.

The mistake would be to assume that there is some important meaning in these effects and then allow yourself to become fearful, distracted, or entertained by these things. These tendencies are perfectly exemplified by the experience of an acquaintance who had ingested some peyote, a hallucinogenic cactus, for fun.

He found himself surrounded by a troop of young, naked, dancing women. He quite enjoyed this hallucination, but after a few minutes of it, the scene vanished, and he confronted the powerful spirit of the cactus. The power and intensity of this spirit was such that the individual was knocked out of his sexual haze and into total rapt attention. The spirit demanded to know what his question was. My friend felt like he needed to have a worthy question quickly or he would feel the wrath of this spirit for wasting its time. Suddenly and without thought, he asked, "What is the purpose of life?" The spirit was pleased with this question and gave him an undeniably valuable answer.

This spirit did my friend a great service by slapping him out of his distraction while still offering him a chance to learn further. In most cases, getting distracted is the end of any learning as the motivation becomes entertainment, not spiritual unfoldment.

Memory

After the Isness inspirience (Chapter 5), all I wanted to do was to get back to that divine place that I called Isness. The memory was always on my mind, constantly being compared to my daily life. The effect of holding this memory was extremely negative. It caused stress and did not allow for the least bit of enjoyment because my experiences just could not compare to Isness. The memory of Isness had become a millstone around my neck.

One day, while taking a therapy lesson from my instructor in Japan, I told him about the Isness inspirience and how it was constantly on my mind. I hoped that he would have some good advice. Because of arrogance, I was also expecting that he would be impressed by the inspirience, but contrary to my expectation he told me, "I recommend that you forget it." I was stunned. That was the last thing I thought he'd say. It felt like blasphemy. Honestly, I was a little insulted because he did not appear to value something that I held in such high esteem. I did not want to be rude or argue with him, so I let it drop. It's my policy, however, to be open to any criticism or advice, so for the next several months, I allowed his comment to simmer within, being open to the possibility that there was something of value in what he said. Little by little, the memory of the Isness inspirience slipped out of the forefront of my mind and stopped tainting everything. Life became beautiful again, and I was able to be more present.

My mistake was equating memory with actuality. Most students are doing this very same thing early on in their meditation practice, I find. They have a great session and then, for a number of sessions afterward, try to remake the prior experience. This blocks them from being present and their energy field does not expand. They may believe that they are in a harmonious frequency, but anyone who has the eyes to see knows that they are actually tuned to the mind. Let memories be memories, and do not try to relive them. Toss out all expectation, and be open to all possibilities at all times. This is the way to have true inspirience in the moment.

Psychic Senses

Words of warning: we are not trying to develop psychic senses here. We are merely resolving inner darkness and revealing what is innate once the veil of conditionality is removed. Psychic senses do not help reveal Isness because Isness is not localized in any specific realm, nor has it an image or a definition, so there is no way to sense it. In the event that a psychic sense opens up, do not feed it with attention. Instead, keep attention spread evenly in a relaxed fashion.

Sometimes an individual will inadvertently open up a psychic doorway by focusing on a specific sense and then be unable to close it again. One such student opened up clairaudience by paying too much attention to the sense of hearing in the meditation because of the ease with which he thought he could meditate if he focused exclusively on sound.

Since his attention was focused on sound as opposed to all senses globally, and because he was predisposed to clairaudience, he quickly opened up that psychic sense and found that he could not stop it during that meditation. It surprised him that he found he could hear the sounds of a party that had taken place in that room many years earlier, glasses clinking, drunken people chatting at full volume. As a meditator he became totally distracted by something completely useless for his goal of tuning to consciousness.

We tested him and found that he was unable to do basic movements that one can do effortlessly in a balanced meditation, so his over-focus on sound had imbalanced him and allowed disharmony to settle in the body. Feeding psychic senses will tune one in the direction of disharmony due to conditioned focus upon a certain direction, sense, place, or thing rather than toward the whole of all that is.

Fortunately, after getting this student back to total awareness, he could feel the difference and chose to continue tuning toward Isness rather than playing psychically. The next session, he did not have any problem with clairaudience.

Many new students mistakenly assume that my awareness of their energy field is a psychic ability, but in reality it's nothing of the sort. It's purely through tuning to Isness that I perceive it. I am convinced that anyone who resolves their divisions can do the very same thing.

Psychotropics

Warning: Consumption of psychotropics is potentially dangerous because of the possibility that someone with an allergy or illness could be harmed or even killed via the use of these substances. The author is in no way recommending that anyone take hallucinogenic substances of any kind.

I generally caution against taking any psychotropics (hallucinogenic substances) unless one feels deeply pulled to do so. The *natem* experience in the Amazon was extremely valuable to me, and were it not for that ceremony I might not yet be at a point where this book could be written. The *natem* ceremony sped up my unfoldment process dramatically — not because the medicine did the work for me, but instead because it helped guide me in a direction that allowed me to work out the hints received through the vision.

I have heard of many people who have had profound spiritual understandings from the use of other psychotropic plants, so clearly psychotropics can be an extremely valuable tool in the process of spiritual unfoldment. And for some individuals who are extremely caught up in themselves, and who simply need a plant intervention to break a negative cycle and give them some insight into their state of mind, psychotropics may be an important tool, because a lot of individuals who are in such negative, self-absorbed states will not be able to meditate or will be unwilling even to try.

That said, there is a danger to using any substance for revelation. What I have noticed and warn against is that because the information comes easily, it often stops there. What I mean is that we may gain a very interesting story and some spiritual information from the experience, but often it does not significantly alter the structures and choices of our lives. If one gains useful guidance through any vehicle, that is only the beginning. Do the homework of incorporating the guidance into daily life in order to complete the circle. If this critical step is omitted, then how was the ceremony different than using any other type of drug for entertainment or escape?

The most dangerous aspect of using psychotropics is that, almost without exception, we begin to feel that we need them in order to have spiritual insight. This means that in our daily lives we feel disconnected, and therefore we start to rely on a hallucinogen to get that spiritual feeling. This is a crutch if there ever was one. Instead of realizing that human beings are born with all they need to tune to consciousness, we may begin to feel that we need the hallucinogen in order to make a connection. This idea is not much different from that of needing a priest to be the mediator between us and God, a crippling limitation.

It all comes down to motivations and intentions. If one feels pulled to take a psychotropic, and it feels right to do so, if the intentions are purely for gaining insight and healing, and there is a firm determination to follow through with the process by incorporating any valuable lessons into one's life, then it's probably going to be an incredible learning opportunity. That said, if we make space for the meditation practice as outlined above and have the right intentions, we will probably have no need for psychotropic substances to gain spiritual insight, and with persistence the meditations will harmonize our daily lives. Even meditation is a tool that we must not allow to become a crutch. Eventually we will transcend all tools.

The Savior

Throughout human culture the savior archetype is ubiquitous. We can see this tendency in ancient cultures through such stories as King Arthur and his sword Excalibur, and through religions including Buddhism and Christianity. In modern culture, we have added greatly to this archetype through movie characters such as Superman, Luke Skywalker in *Star Wars*, Gandalf from *The Lord of the Rings,* and Neo from *The Matrix*. Add to these all the video games in which we play the role of the savior, such as *The Elder Scrolls*, *Half-Life*, *Final Fantasy*, and *Deus Ex*, to name but a few.

I commonly hear people say, "I am a very spiritual person," or "I'm not a very spiritual person." Both of these statements come from a fundamental misunderstanding that anyone can be any more or less spiritual than anyone else. Everyone and everything is equally spiritual because everything is of Isness. The difference between people is merely their degree of realization of what lies at the core. But everyone has the potential to realize Isness. Consider this statement: "I am very spiritual." What frequency does this statement arise from? Mind, of course, because it is comparative to other people, whom the speaker sees as being less spiritual. What about: "I am the chosen one"; "I am the Savior"; "I am the Christ" – what is the root that gives expression to these statements? Mind, right? These statements stem from identifications. If we pay attention, we will realize that there is a feeling in the body that goes with these statements. Resolve the feeling in the body, tune to consciousness, and be at peace. It's profoundly simple. But thanks to its simplicity, it is elusive to the mind.

The truth is we are all here to realize Isness. It's not a race, so some of us may appear to realize before others, but if we truly have realized, we also realize that time is an illusion of the multiverse. From the perspective of Isness there is only potentiality expressing in the eternal moment as the multiverse. From this perspective, are not all of us fully realized in the eternal moment? Tune to the timeless, and make it your abode.

Imagine having a vision wherein you are declared to be anointed to teach a path to graduation that would help humanity to tune to consciousness. How might you feel after this? After the Isness inspirience, I was clearly reminded that I had a mission on Earth to help bring the awareness of Isness within to the people of the world. I began to feel as though I were somehow special in the world even though, paradoxically, I could see that Isness is throughout all that is and in the heart of everyone. After being shown the specifics of my purpose on Earth through the Amazon vision, the feeling of "I'm the chosen one" was even more palpable. Although I could see that each person has the very same core, which is Isness, somehow hearing that I was anointed for the purpose of revealing that to humanity made me feel even more "special."

There was a great struggle within me, as two voices waged war.

One said, "You are no different than anyone else." The other said, "You are special". Whenever I heard that second voice, a feeling of superiority and arrogance began to flood my body. This identification brought about a feeling of great separation because it meant that I was superior to others in some unseen way; I was the authority. Thankfully, there was also the feeling that all people had this same potential, so I worked to resolve "special" whenever it arose. It was an identification, and a powerful one at that. Through teaching I have clearly seen that each person not only has the core of Isness within, but they are able to access and express it to an astonishing degree in a very short period of time.

One individual told me, "I feel such divine states of love. It is truly amazing. Why me?" This question, of course, is covering over a deeper question, which is "Am I special? Am I chosen?" In reply to this student I simply answered, "Why not you?" I planted a seed in the person that hopefully grows into a different question: "Why not everyone?" Be ever watchful of spiritual arrogance. It is an identification that knocks a great many spiritual leaders off the path. Remember, we are all of Isness with the very same potentiality. Some may realize Isness before others from a timeline perspective, but ultimately all potentiality is actuality in the eternal moment, right? So, why not everyone?

~Chapter 14~
Resolving Disharmony

Just as two legs help a human to walk, so do two tools help us to move in balance in the initial stages of unfoldment. The first tool is the meditation that I have already outlined. The second tool is the releasing process, which is called Dance of the Self. What I will teach here is something learned many years ago that has proven to be essential in the unfoldment process.

The Observation Meditation as taught is extremely powerful, and it will bring up darkness to be resolved. If you meditate but do not have a tool to resolve the darkness that arises, it's akin to closing all the windows in your house and then sweeping the floor. You're going to kick up all that dust and not be able to breathe. Dance of the Self is a method to open the main windows of the self – the physical window, the emotional window, and the mental window – to allow the uplifted dust to exit.

Dance of the Self

Every day set aside 10 to 15 minutes of time to consistently use for Dance of the Self. Go into a private space such as your bedroom or bathroom, where you know you will not be disturbed. Reflect on your day and notice any disharmony within yourself, during interactions with other people, or related to any events. What we are looking for is disharmony within ourselves, not in other people. For example, you were annoyed when speaking with the person in the adjacent cubicle at work. All mental disharmony resides within the body, so when you remember the interaction with that individual, feel where the disharmony is in the body. Once you find it, forget the story, and focus lightly and lovingly on the feeling in the body.

Once in touch with the feeling, allow the body to move it out. You might find that the body wants to shake and the fists want to clench, or it might feel like dry-heaving or any number of other things. Let the body do whatever is necessary to channel that disharmony out. To amplify the flow, we can add vocalization as well. As your attention is on the disharmonious feeling within the body, the voice will also be tuned to that feeling; therefore, it may not be a beautiful voice, but it should not use words; instead, just keep it to basic sounds. Let this process continue until the feeling is totally drained. When it's finished, you will often feel extremely clear, as if you just meditated. This is good. If there is more to release, just locate the emotion in the body and release some more.

An easy and effective way to test whether there is still more negative energy to be released is to go back to the memory of the day on which you noticed the original disharmony. If, when remembering the story, there is still disharmony, then there is more available for release. As soon as you find the energy in the body, set aside the story again and just "dance" and "sing" out the darkness.

Dance of the Self is an extremely effective method of releasing disharmony that would otherwise unconsciously spill into our daily life. This spillage causes tremendous relationship strife, which we can circumvent through intentional release in a private, safe place. Just remember not to become overfocused or willful in this process. Never more than 10 percent.

After I was taught Dance of the Self, I did it religiously every night. I began in the shower because I was self-conscious of any noises that I might make while vocalizing. I didn't want my wife to hear it and think I was crazy. It was only about a month into the process before I started to see the positive effects of Dance of the Self.

Through this process, I became aware of an issue that I had previously not recognized. For years, probably all the way back to my childhood, I had a tremendous anxiety that would flood my body and leave me unable to relax while walking. It felt like an engine revving up in my chest, and anxiety would radiate out to the rest of my body. It drove me to constant movement. My foot would tap constantly. I felt like I had to fast-walk everywhere I went. Sometimes the anxiety would get so intense that I had the overwhelming and unconscious desire to run, which is to say that even if I tried to walk calmly, within a minute or two I would be fast-pacing, then running, and realize it only after the fact. If there was no way for me to burn out that anxiety by running, then it would come forth at people through general grumpiness and emotional reactivity.

About a month after doing Dance of the Self consistently, that anxiety disappeared. I found myself able to enjoy a nice stroll home in the evening, and my foot stopped tapping constantly. I was able to relax, which was an entirely new thing for me, and this benefit taught me the profound value of Dance of the Self.

There were many days when only minor darkness was released during my dancing, but I continued doing Dance of the Self regardless. Other times the release was so powerful that it felt as if my body was possessed because of the overwhelming intensity of the energy. After dancing, I always had more clarity.

This kind of dogged persistence is vital to finding success in any endeavor worth doing. It's like drilling for oil. The drill may have to go down quite a ways before it hits a major pocket of oil, right? In the same way, you must go through the dirt days of minor oil to eventually hit a large pocket. When you hit a big pocket of darkness, it will feel as if you are possessed, so powerful is the energy coming through. Just let it come without interfering or judging.

If we find that we suffer from self-consciousness that prevents us from releasing, then that is the first thing to dance out. Notice the location in the body where the energy of self-consciousness hides, and then dance it out.

After a big release it may feel as if there is no disharmony remaining, and it may be true for that day. But rest assured there is much more down there than we can imagine. Just keep at it, day in and day out, without skipping. The only mistake we can make here is the mistake of not doing Dance of the Self.

I just can't bring myself to do Dance of the Self. It feels strange, and sometimes I get fearful just before I start.

It's not you who feels it's strange, nor is it you who is fearful, but those are both things that can be danced out. When those feelings come up, meditate and then inquire into them, and you will see that they are not you. Many people will feel embarrassed to do Dance of the Self even in a totally private space. This embarrassment is not really them; it's an identification that we have empowered and that has taken the pilot's seat of our mind. Feel into this embarrassment. When you are ready, dance out embarrassment first.

What do you mean, it's not me who feels it's strange?

When I say "you," I am not referring to your personality or to the self, but instead to the unconditioned, eternal, undefined you. This is the actual you that never changes, never ages, and does not suffer. This is the you that will be revealed through the process of unfoldment.

I get so angry sometimes that there is no way that I can stop it. What should I do?

If anger is such a volatile identification for us that it immediately takes over and controls us, then we need to become very proactive with regard to anger. Spend time each evening dancing out anger proactively so that this identification is not so highly pressurized.

We also want to look into the feeling of anger in the body with curiosity. When we do this, we may realize that it's not really us that is getting angry, although we may have believed this to be the case for a long time. Couple that with proactive dancing, and we may find that anger does not reach such volatile levels so quickly, which means that we may be able to make calm, productive choices even under pressures that would usually stimulate the identification of anger. Then we can choose not to allow the identification to express at an inappropriate time. We separate ourselves from the situation and do Dance of the Self to release the energy.

In most cases of extreme anger, I have found that the anger is just covering over a deeper hurt. Oftentimes, anger covers over shame or a feeling of vulnerability combined with pride due to being violated in some very emotionally painful way when we were children. That said, we never want to assume anything, so we will look into anger with curiosity in order to open the door for insight. Who knows what lies beneath?

You have said that we should not try to push away or escape from identifications or darkness. But it seems to me that Dance of the Self is just another way of pushing away.

Well, being honest, that boiling-over energy is going to come out one way or another, but it's better that it comes out at a time of our choosing rather than unconsciously coming out on other people. Ideally we would be able to remain in unconditioned love, which resolves darkness directly. However, since that requires a level of stability that a person new to this process does not usually have, Dance of the Self is a necessary tool to help get us to the level of stability at which unconditioned love does the work.

I can't bring myself to do the vocal aspect of Dance of the Self. It's just not me.

The statement "It's just not me" raises the question, "what is you?" This is a perfect example of self-identification, in which we have put a definition on the self, and that definition becomes the limiting factor. As you define, so you limit. Any more than "I am," and we get into trouble. That being stated, we have to work from where we are, which is to some degree or another in self-definition, whether we realize it or not. We do not wish to become willful, so we'll just do what we can with Dance of the Self and move forward one step at a time. So, in this case, just omit the voice until the self content has softened to the point at which the voice can be added.

I tried Dance of the Self a few times, and I am not yet free of my issue. I don't think it's helping.

We must be careful that our motivation is not stemming from a desire to escape an issue. If the actual motivation is unfoldment, then there is a positivity that can bring us to peace; but if the desire is to escape an issue, then darkness is the guiding force, because the desire to escape is also an identification that leads us into more disharmony. Take some time to meditate on both your conscious and unconscious motivations. You may find that observing resolves the desire to escape. Finally, nothing of real value comes easily.

Investment into the process will be necessary for anything of value to occur.

Negative Atmospheres

One night I was sleeping over at the home of a friend, Jane, on the living room floor. Earlier in the evening there had been a healing session with a dozen or so people present. Gatherings like this were commonly held in the living room. Around six o'clock in the morning, I was startled awake by a presence right next to me. I looked to my left, and there was a man sitting with his knees folded beneath him, gazing into my chest.

He had the exact appearance of a trusted friend. It was strange that he would be there, not only because of the early hour, but also because he did not know Jane. I looked into his eyes, and a current of dread ran through my body. This was not my friend; it was pure evil. I tried to move away from this spirit, but my body was totally frozen. He smiled maliciously at me and began to pull energy from my torso. I was being drained. But worse than being drained was the feeling of helplessness.

During this paralysis I could move my eyes, and what I noticed was that the woman whose house this was had walked right past me into the kitchen to prepare breakfast. She was a professional psychic, so I tried to call out to her in hopes that she would be able to help me, but no sound would pass my lips.

Suddenly I realized that it was my fear that was empowering this spirit. The more fear I felt, the more powerful it became. With that, my fear turned to determination, and I was able to conjure up enough clarity to break the binds. The spirit's face betrayed his surprise as my body was freed. He immediately disappeared, and I could no longer feel his presence. Immediately, I was free of the paralysis. I got up and told the story to Jane, who was in the kitchen.

This could simply have been a dream, some might assert. Some may interpret this experience as being of an evil spirit, then assume that this spirit was there because the work being done there was evil, but that would be an incorrect assumption. This experience was not the result of some evil work that had been occurring in the living room. Instead it came from a crucial oversight and lack of awareness.

It wasn't until many years later that I understood the dynamics of what happened that evening.

After some months of doing Dance of the Self, I awoke suddenly in the middle of the night, feeling an evil presence in the room. I looked up and saw, just above my face, a dark form staring down at me. I awakened just before the paralysis I felt earlier, and the spirit immediately disappeared. I was a bit surprised by this encounter, but because it had happened before in my life I understood that fear was not a valuable response.

Again, about a month later, the same thing happened. Then several weeks later, then a week, then several times a week and finally five times in one night, each spirit progressively more powerful than the last. I was utterly exhausted. I knew without a doubt that this was a serious problem that needed to be dealt with right away. No matter how aware we are, if we awaken enough times during the night, eventually we will fail to wake due to exhaustion.

Clearly, I thought, the strategy was to exhaust me and take my energy while I was asleep. I didn't think I had enough disharmony within me to draw darkness in this way, so I was somewhat confused. I thought about the issue all day while at work, searching for a solution. There are a lot of teachings that say we should put up spiritual protection, but I felt that shielding is a crutch that compensates for our inner corruption, the fuel that actually attracts negative spirits. These spirits are like flies; if you take out the garbage, you don't have many flies around.

That night when I got home, I went into the bedroom and meditated on the issue. My awareness shifted, and I found myself scanning the room, looking for disharmony. My eyes stopped at the spot where I always did Dance of the Self. I had been sloughing off darkness night after night for months on that spot, and it just sat there like so much garbage. And like garbage, it was attracting flies. That spot had become a beacon of disharmony in the house. I had put the energy there, so I was responsible for it, and that was the cause of these negative experiences.

I understood that I needed to clean up that energy. Since I could feel the dark energy with my eyes and hands, I started sending it love and transforming it into positive, light energy. Little by little that darkness resolved to positivity. I understood that one of the laws of consciousness is that what comes through our minds, we are responsible for, and until every last bit of it is resolved to Isness, we are not free. I made a habit of going through this healing process after every Dance of the Self session. The negative visitations ceased.

The more we walk the spiritual path, the more identifications will come up within us, causing us disharmony, unless we have a method to release and resolve this darkness. If we release identifications without resolving that energy to purity, then we will create a negative environment wherever we have been sloughing off that disharmony.

There are certain spiritual techniques in which we transfer inner darkness into items or onto paper and then burn them. Burning separates us from that disharmony, dispersing it over a large range, but it does not resolve the energy back to an unconditioned state of purity. Since we have not taken the important step of resolving the energy, we are still responsible for it. Thus, burning only increases the amount of time that the energy is separated from us, but it will return because we created it. Taking personal responsibility is the key to resolving disharmony.

Resolution Process

Once your dancing is finished, step out of the room and spend a few minutes to acclimate to being without that disharmony. Because we have carried and identified ourselves with that energy over time, it is effectively camouflaged as us. It's as if it carries our scent, and, therefore, we can't smell it. Other sensitive people may be able to, but we cannot. So, by separating from it for a bit, we increase the odds that we can perceive it as if it were not our own.

After a few minutes, go back into the room as if you were totally innocent and pure, and clean up the place where the energy was released. Because the energy is negative, it will be heavy and naturally fall to the floor. It may extend up from the floor several feet or higher depending on how much and how powerful the release was. Direct loving attention to that area and feel that energy becoming light and clear, rising up to Heaven. Now, in truth, Heaven is in no one particular place, so up is not really where it's at, but we understand that light things float up and heavy things drop down, so we can use this associated understanding as a way to communicate spiritually that we want this darkness to resolve to unconditioned purity. Keep directing love to that spot until the area has a light, fresh atmosphere.

It won't take very long before you find your own personal way of resolving energy, but the key point is to keep it simple and pure without adding unnecessary steps to the process. Most importantly, do not judge, fear, or push away the energy. All energy, even that which has been tainted with darkness, ultimately comes from Isness, and it's not our place to judge it. Our job is only to resolve it and to remain loving and peaceful.

Clean up after Dance of the Self every day, without fail if at all possible. If you skip a day, make sure to do it the next day or the disharmony that sloughed off will start to create a dark atmosphere in that space. Eventually, you may end up with an intensely dark spot that attracts disharmonious experiences. The law is that we are responsible for the energy that we put out. If we do not resolve it, it will create disharmony. Releasing and resolving darkness to Isness is the way to make consistent progress.

~Part 3~
Daily Unfoldment

The process of spiritual unfoldment is first and foremost a process of tuning to Isness. Gradually, through this process, impedimentary perspectives that we have held slough away like dead skin, and with each layer released and resolved, a little more light is able to shine through, allowing further insight into our true natures. In this way, unfoldment is an undoing and unbinding process that reveals the very core, which is Isness.

In this section, I discuss many of the challenges that the unfolding individual is likely to resolve in the process. As most of us will be drawn to a teacher at some point, we discuss the student/teacher relationship thoroughly, as well as some of the fundamental, insightful teachings of my teachers. We also discuss the various ways in which Isness may provide hints that serve to awaken us, so that we may best take advantage of them when they occur. Then we look at methods for improving the health of the body, for without a healthy, vibrant body, the conscious unfoldment process is far more challenging. We explore our relationship with the body itself, with food, with exercise, and with the elements. Next, we look at various aspects of caring for the mind, for when the mind is out of balance, our lives spiral out of control, potentially derailing the active unfoldment process and causing a great deal of disharmony. Finally we address common difficulties with purpose, forgiveness, and prayer, and we shed new light on these vital human processes. This section also includes some basic advice on the unfoldment process, as well as things to consider releasing. This is your process, so you are welcome to hang on to anything for as long as you want. When you are ready to release something, it will begin to happen. Until then, play with what you are willing to release and resolve it. In this way we unfold without feeding willfulness.

~Chapter 15~
Teachers

In my life, I have been blessed to train with some of the very best teachers in Japan, ones tasked with carrying ancient traditions into the modern world. Their level of experience is deep, and much of what they pass on largely goes unrecognized and unvalued in the world, as what they teach has largely been relegated to the bygone days of the samurai.

Although these ancient traditions are of a martial nature — focused on fighting with swords, staves, and knives, as well as the unarmed body — there is much that can be learned from seeking to quiet the body and the mind under the pressure of potential injury or death. Furthermore, the depth and intricacies of these arts require the practitioner to explore deeply the workings of the mind and the body. When we train genuinely to discover the gaps of the mind and the weaknesses of the body and to eliminate those gaps and weaknesses, we may begin to open a path to realization.

There are countless things that I learned from such training, but most of them can be understood only through direct physical contact and experience with the body. To speak or write of them would trivialize the teachings. For that reason I have not dealt much in this book with these training methods, even though they were pivotal to my unfoldment process. That said, there are some core teachings that are absolutely pivotal to the unfoldment process, and that can be conveyed through the medium of a book.

There is a certain wisdom that comes from cutting away all that is unnecessary to maximize effortless efficiency. I'd like to share some of the wisdom of my teachers, who have spent most of their lives studying the mind and the body and refining their arts to as near perfection as is humanly possible.

The Student/Teacher Relationship

In much of the world these days there is very little respect for teachers, which causes a negative environment in most schools. Teachers are paid little and are often overlooked or undervalued by society. A saying that sums up the attitude goes, "Those who cannot do, teach." This is very unfortunate. As a result of the low status of teachers, the forceful nature of school, the factory model that schools embrace, and the focus on testing, most individuals have very unhealthy associations with learning and with teachers.

The relationship between a teacher and the student on the path of unfoldment is quite distinct from comparable relationships on other paths. In old-world countries, some traditions of discipleship and apprenticeship remain intact. We can see this demonstrated with regard to certain schools of ancient martial arts and certain monasteries. These schools focus on passing along traditions and certain skill sets, many of which incorporate spiritual training methods, but as these schools are focused primarily on a skill set or fixed tradition, it's necessarily a different environment than that of a school specific to spiritual unfoldment. We must bear this difference in mind when we study any tradition.

Many individuals on the path of unfoldment will be pulled to study under teachers and mentors of possibly a variety of traditions and skills. The teachers serve not only to pass on information and bring out the very best in their students, but also to inspire us to surpass their level. If such teachers are far along the path of unfoldment, just being in their presence helps to raise us out of mind and into consciousness.

With regard to formalities, students should address a teacher by title to show respect, unless the teacher specifies otherwise. The student needs to have a deep interest in the teacher, to the point of being captivated, because everything about that teacher is a potential hint that can be learned from. That said, the student must not worship the teacher nor must the student be blind to the teacher's shortcomings. Instead, the student observes and learns, being conscientious of what is of value as well as what is not, all the while showing deep respect.

The student and the teacher decide on a training schedule, and both abide by it, arriving on time and practicing with enthusiasm. Although the student deeply respects the teacher, he or she must never act against conscience even at the direction of the teacher. If the teacher does not accept this stance, then the student in search of unfoldment may be better off finding a new teacher. A student is polite, listens openly, and practices what the teacher teaches without trying to demonstrate outside methods or otherwise show off. After training, the student cleans and tidies up the training space.

Students who fail to show respect, who are repeatedly late for no real reason, or who cannot keep to a training schedule might want to consider looking into their motivations because they are, in all likelihood, wasting everyone's time and energy. The student pays all required fees in a timely manner so as not to unnecessarily burden the teacher. If the individual is unable to attend a scheduled class or will knowingly be late, they need to contact their teacher in a timely manner. If the student wishes to take a prolonged break, it is proper to inform the teacher. If the student intends to withdraw, it's also proper to let the teacher know this respectfully, either personally or in writing. If one fails to do these simple things, one is unworthy to study anything of depth.

Much more is required of senior students intending to become teachers of a path. They need to be willing to enthusiastically support the teacher in training activities and seminars, and with matters of the school or organization. They may be asked to handle some aspects of training lower-level students. This is part of their preparation for becoming teachers themselves. In such a case, they must always defer to the main teacher and not demonstrate things they have not been encouraged to teach. They must never seek to bolster their position or ego.

The important thing to remember is that the school is not there just for the sake of the teacher — which is to say that the school is often there to represent an entire lineage of hard-earned wisdom that stretches back many generations, possibly hundreds or thousands of years. Students who join such a school are part of that lineage and therefore should be aware that they are representing all of those individuals. Such a student should use the high standards of the lineage as a motivation to improve and find the dignity within.

Blame

There was one fellow student at the dojo to whom I had much difficulty applying *aiki* techniques, even after I already had my master's license. I remember that one night, after training with this student, I mumbled privately to Sensei that I didn't think this student was attacking honestly. He looked down for a moment thoughtfully and replied, "I think maybe it's something that you are projecting which is causing this person to attack in ways that feel strange to you." After letting that sink in for a moment, he continued, "I have come to understand that I can't improve if I blame other people. I try to remember that whatever happens is a reflection of the energy that I am projecting."

It is so interesting to see what happens to the mind when we are tuned to a high frequency of harmony. During this time, we will wonder why we get upset when our spouse does this or says that. When viewed from a frequency of consciousness, we will realize how petty we are about many things when we are tuned to mind. Believe it or not, it's possible to have such a high frequency of consciousness that there can be no abuse. But we may not be tuned to this high frequency all the time, so there can be vulnerability.

It is important to realize that any frequency of mind is open to abuse, so even "good" people who are tuned to mind are open to abusiveness if they put themselves in a position for it to occur. Years ago many a wife was blamed when her husband beat her. People would say, "It takes two to argue" or "You must have done something to anger him." But really, she was just tuned to mind, not unconditioned love, while he was expressing an abuse-identification on her. If we have a spouse who is identified with abusiveness and acts it out, and we are unable to tune to a frequency beyond abusiveness, then we may ask ourselves if maintaining the relationship is actually beneficial for all involved. If it's not, then separating may be the best option. To remain in a toxic relationship is not really a sane choice, is it? The desire to remain in such a relationship may indicate some strong identifications of our own. To remain in the relationship will pull both individuals into a low frequency of mind. This is not a judgment against such a choice, however, because the individual may need that experience to understand the futility of it just as I did.

Once, a self-described psychic, after having met me for the first time, said she had a message for me. I went to her house later and she gave me the message. The message was that I was dating a girl who was toxic for me and that I would be well advised to leave her. I felt that the message was true, but I loved the girl, and I believed that I could help her, so I did not follow the advice. In the end I was not able to help, and I realized it was spiritual arrogance that led me to believe I could fix her. We could say that this psychic had given me good advice, but in reality I needed that experience to realize not only that I could not fix someone but that the very desire, in my case, stemmed from arrogance. If I had not learned that lesson, then even if I had left her, I would still be attracting the same type of toxic relationship now, which is how life works. So from this perspective, how can we say that anyone's advice is correct? Sometimes we need disharmonious experiences until we no longer need them. This is perfectly normal and natural for those tuned to mind.

There may be options that come through meditation. If they feel right, then go with those options. Ultimately we do not want to turn life into an "if, then" routine, right? Tune to unconditioned love and look into the issue, and you may find better answers than anyone could ever give you.

Malicious Mind

Once, Sensei stopped during practice and said, "Never try to throw people because it will make your mind sick. It's wrong to try to throw people." It struck me as a strange comment since we are always throwing people in this training. Later that afternoon we had a party, so I took the opportunity to ask Sensei what he meant by his admonition not to throw people. He seemed pleased with my question and filled my sake cup. "In *Daito-Ryu* [the name of the martial art style], we use *aiki*, which is to say, we use harmony. To try to throw someone is a malicious intent, don't you think? That is not harmony, is it? Instead of trying to throw someone, just move your body here or there in harmony. If the person is attacking you, they will naturally fall down, even though that was not your intention. Just move in harmony."

Since that time, I have found that it's also malicious to try to change people. It's better to remain in harmony and allow inspiration to do the work. Harmony is inspiring. Of course, that does not mean that we can't make a suggestion here or there when asked, but remove force and expectation from the equation, and, of course, remain in harmony.

I have found this to be most challenging with regard to family relationships because of the degree to which they are bound in expectation. For this reason, family relationships are great learning opportunities. You may think you have the perfect answer to solve someone's "problem," but they reject it outright because, really, they do not want to solve the problem; they just want to complain. Or maybe they do not see the cause of the problem as having anything to do with their own energetic projection; instead, they would like to blame others. In such cases your suggestion will not be accepted, and if you push it, there will be argument or avoidance.

Therefore, whenever making a suggestion we put it out there lightly, and if it's rejected, let it be. At some point, another opportunity may arise to make another suggestion, at which time we may put it out there again, but without expectation. It's like casting out our fishing line. We do not expect a fish to bite every time we cast, do we? Of course not. We cast without expectation, right? This is the way to communicate with people while remaining tuned to consciousness.

Many times people who ask for advice really are not wanting any advice at all, but instead are looking for a shoulder to cry on. It's up to you if you wish to lend your shoulder or not. Beware, for sympathy only feeds identifications, and pity helps no one. In the event that we give advice, the temptation to make the person see the solution may be strong. We may feel that we are helping them by pushing them to see it. But, in truth, other people are not our responsibility, and we cannot make them do anything. They have their own free will, and it's wise to respect that.

If we push too far and it comes back to hit us in the face, then it's only proper that we apologize for being pushy. If this happens, instead of digging in further, apologize and forgive immediately once you realize the disharmony that pushing has stimulated. If the individual continues down the path of disharmony and their problem gets them into trouble, be aware that there is no need for you to feel bad about not being able to help because feeling bad does not help anyone. We can love and care for people and not feel bad when things do not go well for them. Instead, we remain in a calm state, ready to be of assistance when the opportunity is ripe. At some point, their situation may get so uncomfortable for them that they will honestly seek help, at which time they may listen.

Authenticity

Although I have been extremely fortunate with my teachers, not every teacher is a good, healthy demonstration of humanity. I have seen many teachers over the years, and I have come to the realization that the majority are selfish and egotistical.

It seems to me that many teachers pretend that they are wise sages and all-knowing masters, afraid of showing their humanity. One such teacher even told his own mother, who was not a student of his, that she must call him Grand Master. She called him lots of things, but Grand Master was not one of them. Many teachers seem like they are mere caricatures of people. I have seen many times that this condition leads to abuse of all sorts that students then pay forward to those lower on the totem pole, both in and out of the dojo.

In the West, there are so many "Masters" who buy and exchange ranks, certificates, and titles. I have received several letters from "Masters" requesting that I give them rank in the arts I teach in exchange for rank in their arts. There was no interest in training; they just wanted the rank so they could add to their collection and bragging rights. This is just another example of a lack of integrity and authenticity.

I suppose such teachers are trying to live up to the Hollywood image of a "Master," and so they try to bolster their position and stoke their image. Liberated individuals do not identify themselves as being masters, and people walking the path of unfoldment with integrity know there is still much more to know and understand than they have yet to touch upon, so how can people call themselves master and maintain integrity?

Be authentic; admit mistakes and imperfections when they show up. Apologize authentically when an apology is in order. This is part of being human, and this is what inspires. At the same time observe teachers carefully, and note any lack of integrity so as not to be led astray. Live with integrity, heart as light as a feather, attracting other human beings seeking that same lightness.

Complacency

When I joined my first dojo in Japan, not knowing anything, I asked Sensei, "How close to perfection are you in your technique?" He replied, "I never believe in 100 percent because if I believe in 100 percent then there is nothing more to understand, no more depth to explore. In reality, there is always more to uncover and to understand. So I always try for an ever-expanding 97 percent, leaving room to believe that there is still 3 percent remaining that I have yet to discover. Then I am eager to find that last 3 percent. And no matter how much my understanding grows, there is always another 3 percent left to discover, because as my understanding grows, so does the remaining 3 percent."

The realization that there is always more to understand is very helpful in the unfoldment process. I am constantly asking questions in silence, seeking insight. I write the questions and the answers and then look back on that information repeatedly to ask deeper questions still. No matter how much I realize, there is always more to be understood, more to refine.

Remain Behind

Once, while I had dinner with my teacher after training, he spoke of the tendency for some students to believe that they should be given a higher rank than they actually deserve because they are high ranked in other arts or traditions. He said, "They have a strong desire to demand recognition for their accomplishments even though they do not understand the art I am teaching. I think the better way is the exact opposite of this tendency. Your job is to become so effective that others push you up because they feel awkward when compared to you because you are of equal rank with them even though your ability is obviously beyond theirs. In this way, you may be pushed up without ever desiring it, and therefore there is no ego involved. Your job is not to push your way up, but instead it's to perfect, to refine and purify. If you are not pushed up, that is okay too, because you have no ego about it."

This teacher's words are very wise, but it's possible to embrace this philosophy and still have an unconscious identification that creates the desire, unbeknownst to others and even to ourselves, to be at the top. It takes constant observation of the mind to notice this type of identification.

I remember once, about six months after I was given the instructor's license, one of the other students in the dojo took his test for the same license, and I was there as an observer. I felt a strong desire for him to fail the test. I did not want him to pass the test and be equal with me. Suddenly I realized how absurd the feeling was, as it was rooted entirely in mind and carried no harmony whatsoever. I resolved that identification and found myself cheering for this individual, who, fortunately, did pass the test. I would have felt awful had he failed it, knowing that I hadn't completely supported him.

There are many teachers of ancient arts who intentionally withhold knowledge from students in order to keep them down. This desire is entirely of the mind and causes both short-term and long-term disharmony. The immediate effect is that students believe the teacher is naturally superior, that they can never match his or her level. The long-term effect is that key knowledge does not get passed down, and the arts become useless shells of their former glory. If teachers were tuned to consciousness they would see the uselessness of such a selfish desire, and they would desire to train students so that one day they will surpass the teacher's abilities. In this way, the arts get stronger and stronger through the generations. So much ancient knowledge has been lost because of the ego-driven desire of the mind. Only students of ancient arts who have rediscovered some of this lost knowledge will have any idea of how destructive "secrets" have been.

On an emotional level, we have a tendency to compare our lives to those of people who have it worse than us in order to feel better about our own lives. This strategy is entirely of the mind and is indicative of a very low-frequency identification indeed. We can also see that at the lowest frequencies of mind, identifications get upset when others succeed, and thus the desire is to tear down those successful individuals in any way possible. All of these feelings come from a conditioned mind. They do not even exist when the self is fully resolved. Comparisons can never bring any form of stability or joy, but consciousness can.

Butter Over Bread

A sword instructor in Japan used to say that our techniques should be as smooth as spreading warm butter over bread. The idea was to remove any clunky, abrupt, or disharmonious movements so that the techniques become so smooth as to have no telegraphing. In this way, our movements become effectively invisible to the attacker. Although attackers can see the body moving, their minds are unable to feel changes until it's too late.

With regard to unfoldment, we can take this same approach and apply it to the whole of life while removing any sense of an opponent. In this manner, unfoldment will occur quite naturally at a much faster pace. We can use the "spreading butter over bread" feeling when observing the flow of our breath or our pulse to easily notice when disharmony is arising within us, even before there is any recognizable emotion or thought. In this way, we can resolve arising disharmony before it overwhelms us.

A person on the path of unfoldment seeks to become as aware as possible of the workings of their own body and mind in the moment. Since all thinking and feeling is mirrored in the body through the breath, pulse, and tension, we should develop such sensitivity and awareness that we know whenever there is tension in the body. Can you feel the pulse in all parts of the body by mere intention? Can you feel the pulse in your fingers and toes without touching them? Can you feel the pulse in your eyes?

Diligence

I once asked my teacher what it takes to master *aiki*. He paused for a moment and then responded, "Practice every day but do not train yourself inflexibly. Instead train to be flexible and open because, quite naturally, your expression of each technique will change gradually and simplify as you perceive deeper through training. If you just come to class, this is insufficient. Each student who has completed my training has come to class regularly and practiced on their own diligently."

To practice flexibly means to practice without identifying ourselves strongly with the expression of our techniques, which is to say, we do not have the feeling of, "This is how I do it." If we notice this feeling taking root, we might consider softening it to be more like, "This is how I do it at this stage of my understanding. But there may be many other ways of which I am not yet aware." Eventually, there will be no "I" involved. Things will just happen spontaneously, and therefore the expression may be different each and every time.

With regard to practice, I personally did it so much that I trained in my dreams. I practiced on the train, while walking, and when at home. I practiced so much that my wife was annoyed. Eventually I learned to hide my training so that it could happen all the time without anyone noticing. Of course, this level of training occurs only after a great deal of dedication.

With regard to spiritual unfoldment, the process is not really about training or ingraining, but we do need to set a regular schedule for consistent meditation, which resolves darkness within to reveal the fundamental truth at the core of our very being. There is, however, one area in which ingraining is helpful, and that is to develop a habit of taking regular intervals for introspection, because without having curiosity as to what we are feeling and tuning to, we cannot correct the tuning. Add in a regular self-check, so that you will not go too long without one. Then, little by little, decrease the interval between checks until eventually it's constant.

I Can't

One day at the dojo a new student was practicing with Sensei, and after repeated failures of a basic technique this student mumbled in frustration, "It's impossible; I can't." Sensei seemed to understand this person's feelings exactly, for surely he had also been in the same position in his early training. Kindly, he replied to the student, "Never believe that you can't do something. If you say that you can't, then you are right, you can't. But if you say that you can, then even if you can't do it right now, some day, you will be able to do it. You just need to keep at it."

There is a story about a young samurai who was caught in a great storm at sea. Centuries ago a young country samurai named Take went out, off the coast, with his boat for a day of fishing. As he was of low rank, his stipend was insufficient for him to make ends meet for his family. Therefore he supplemented his income of rice with fishing whenever he had the opportunity. He went out into the deep waters, hoping to bring in some large fish for his family.

He left well before sunrise, and after a few hours he was quite far out to sea. He found the spot that he felt he was going to make his catch and lowered his line. The day was warm and comfortable, and before he knew it he was dozing off.

He awoke to the crack of thunder and large drops of cold rain bashing his skin. During his sleep storm clouds silently filled the sky such that he was barely able to see the shore. He knew that the sea became extremely violent during storms like this one, and that being out on the water in such conditions probably meant death. He needed to get to shore before the storm really picked up.

He began rowing as quickly as he could for the dim shore, but the moment he put his oar in the water, the sea began to undulate violently, the waves growing feet at a time. It was too late. He was going to have to hope for a miracle now.

He plowed through wave after wave for an hour, but it seemed he was no closer to the shore. He began tiring, and the thought that he would not make it took root in his mind. He started counting the waves, and as the number rose he lost more of his confidence — the shore still miles away.

Rowing over each wave felt like a monumental task, and the desire to give up grew in his mind. He began to think that the task was impossible and that he would never reach the shore. He found himself wanting to give in to death, to let the sea swallow him up.

It was at this point that he realized that he was allowing the negativity of his mind to overwhelm him, and that counting the waves and trying to guess the distance to the shore was too discouraging. He decided at that point to forget that distant goal and to instead keep things simple. He would tackle each wave one at a time and stop counting them. All he would do was focus on the wave there and then.

Wave after wave came, and with each one he would say to himself, "One." In short order, his mind rested, and his energy was dedicated to the task of navigating the one wave in front of him, no longer projecting to the future and the monumental task ahead. Again and again: "One." "One." "One ...."

That samurai survived because of the Philosophy of One. And with the wisdom of that experience, he eventually became an inspiring leader, teaching others to live powerfully in the present.

When I was training martial arts in Japan, I noticed that within three to six months most students gave up. The art is so difficult that we are certain to fail repeatedly hundreds or thousands of times before having a real taste of success. I remember I spent three years working on just one technique before I could do it well enough to pass my test to begin the next higher curriculum. Can you imagine going five nights a week, for two hours each night, doing the same technique over and over and over, only to fail repeatedly for three straight years? Imagine how many times the voice of the quitter tried to convince me to give up. Whenever I heard that voice, I dismissed it and just kept pressing forward after calming myself. How many people can do that? The truth is that everyone can do it, but few actually do. Most give up because they empower the quitter identification and because they do not embrace the Philosophy of One.

Remaining present in this way is applicable to all avenues of life helping to keep us in the present. My martial arts students often laugh when, after a technique, I say to them, "Just one more." After doing it once more, I repeat, "Just one more." Of course, there is never an end to "Just one more." Through presence, we can accomplish the impossible. Just one more.

In the process of spiritual unfoldment, there will be many times in which we may feel that we are not making any progress or that the road ahead is too difficult to travel. There may be times when we feel down and out, that we can't go on. Remember, there is no shame in crying, but when the tears are over, get back up and start moving again. Just get back up.

Many times while training in Japan I just didn't feel very motivated to go to the dojo, especially after a hard, stressful day of work. The dojo was about an hour from school by train, and getting on the train to go to the dojo, knowing that I still had another hour on the train to get home, could be discouraging. But instead of projecting my mind to the entirety of the trip, I would just focus on getting myself out the door with my gear. If I got that far, I knew I would not turn back. Almost without exception, nights like that afforded the most profound breakthroughs.

Where most people go awry is they give in to the feeling of not wanting to go, and there is the thought, "I'll take tonight off and go tomorrow instead." Those feelings and that thinking don't come from Isness, do they? Get up, grab your gear, and get out the door. If you can make it that far, the momentum will carry you the rest of the way.

This applies to meditation as well. We just make the space for the meditation in our life and follow through every time unless Isness indicates otherwise. If, during the meditation, the mind drifts, don't give up. Just stay there for the allotted time, regardless. We may not realize it, but even though it seems like the time is wasted, it isn't. Half of the process is just making the space and time for the meditation and doing it. Do not expect that each meditation will be comfortable or easy. This will teach us to have follow-through even in times of great difficulty.

~Chapter 16~
Inspiration

The multiverse is founded on self-definition and ignorance, but there is an unseen power throughout all, Isness. Remember, in every breath we take, Isness is there. In every cell of our bodies, there is Isness. In each person we see, in each surface we touch, Isness is there. In the empty spaces, it is there. The key to effective conscious unfoldment is tuning to consciousness in every possible moment of our lives. As we tune ourselves to consciousness, we will find inspiration in our "ordinary" lives because the ordinary becomes extraordinary when perceived through the light of Isness. Here are some helpful hints about how Isness comes into our lives.

Be Mindful of Hints

Every incarnate human being has at least one moment in its existence when Isness gives it a hint as to the possibility. This is a bold statement, but it's true. So the question is, can you remember any of these hints? I have spoken of a number of personal visions and communications with Isness, but now I would like to talk about a more common hint that I think many people may overlook: being in the zone.

We hear professional athletes talk about this phenomenon quite often, but the zone is not limited to professionals or athletes. In "in the zone" moments, grace is flowing through us. Our minds are totally silent, and our bodies just do the right thing at exactly the right moment. It's an absolutely wonderful feeling when it occurs.

My first "in the zone" experience happened when I was in the sixth grade. I was not a good athlete as a child (aside from running), primarily because my body grew too quickly and was ungainly but also because I had no confidence in myself. Being constantly self critical is a crippling disorder, which I had in spades. Anyway, I was usually one of the last kids picked for any sporting team, so I tended to avoid playing sports to spare myself the embarrassment.

One day during lunch break, I was walking along the outdoor basketball court watching a game between some of the best players in my grade. They were one man short of even teams, and since I was the only one watching at the time, I was asked to join. I declined at first, but Rick, the best athlete, an honor-roll student, and a really nice person, kindly came over and asked me if I wouldn't reconsider. I had a strange feeling in my body, and there was a pulling feeling to join them, so I agreed.

I tried to play defense as much as possible, as I didn't want to be a ball handler. I was never any good at making shots in a game under pressure. Unexpectedly, however, the ball ended up in my hands and from that very spot, without any thought, my body launched the ball at the hoop — perfect swish. It was from quite a distance, and everyone was surprised but dismissed it as luck. The game went on, and someone passed the ball to me again.

Jump-shot, swish.

One time is luck, but two in a row means something, so no sooner than my team got the ball, it was in my hands and swish. Over and over and over again, the ball just could not miss. Needless to say, our team won by a wide margin. Everyone huddled around me when the game was over. They were amazed at how good I was. Rick said, "Man, you are better than Magic Johnson." Boy, that felt great. The bell rang, and it was time to head back to class. I thought all the rest of that day and night about that game and began to believe I was a basketball phenom. I guessed that I had found a hidden talent, and I was eager to go out and play again.

We got together at lunch the next day and divvied up teams. I was the top pick for Rick's team. The game started, and the ball went straight to me. I thought I should do the same thing I did the day before, throwing it from wherever I got it, so I tossed the ball at the hoop, and it flew over the backboard. A little later, I got the ball again and – another wide miss. I tried and tried, only to miss every time. It was humiliating. We lost that game, and I was not invited to play again. I was really embarrassed and didn't know what to make of the magic I had just a day before.

It wasn't until years later that I understood what happened that day. I was in "the zone." There was no thought, just Rightness. My body was abuzz with this feeling, and my mind was silent. It was a hint from Isness. Later, of course, my ego kicked in, and I falsely identified myself with the feeling, trying to own it. During the game the following day, all I had going for me was the noise of ego and thought, so we lost the game.

I am sure many people have had similar experiences in one activity or another and probably suffered similar results when they tried it again on another occasion. It's frustrating especially if we egoically try to grab onto the feeling and own it. The key is to stay present and unconcerned with outcomes such as success and failure. Just flow in the present with clarity of spirit allowing the body to be moved.

There are other ways in which Isness gives us hints. We might suddenly feel that we should go somewhere specific, without reason, and then something miraculous happens. We may have an inspiring realization, an answer to something that has been puzzling us for a long time. You may have an extremely vivid dream such as flying, for example, which is of Isness. These things hint as to the freedom that comes from unbinding Soul.

Look back over your life, even into early childhood, and feel through your memories. There are likely to be moments of total wonder and inspiration that catch your attention; chances are, that feeling was one of your hints. If you do not remember anything right away, just keep it in the back of your mind and recheck your memories from time to time. What I have found from many conversations with a great number of individuals is that often they have forgotten these moments because they could not make sense out of them. But after looking back over their lives, again and again, eventually they remember.

Allow Isness to Express

While I was living in Japan, I worked in a private middle school, which is quite an eye-opening experience for a foreigner. You see, in Japanese culture drinking socially and having parties is part and parcel of having friends. Business people, school teachers, club members — almost any adults, really — will find any excuse to get together and drink. In sober moments, everyone is restricted by tight social order and etiquette. But while drinking, such bindings, for the most part, go out the window. So people drink to release stress and get to know each other on a more intimate level, without the shackles of the usual social rules.

These parties tend to be a lot of fun and can get pretty wild as party number one (at a hotel conference room or traditional restaurant) turns into party number two (at a Japanese pub), and, finally, the 2 a.m. taxicab-ride-home party number three (at a hostess club). My school had a long tradition of great parties, and the year-end party was usually the best of them as all the accumulated steam of the year was blown off with the froth of beer and the exhaust of sake. You see, Mr. Shino, our school's vice principal for as long as anyone could remember, was par excellence at getting these parties rolling by taking the stage and shaking his hips to a Rod Stuart karaoke tune.

But that year we had a new principal and a new vice to go with him. Although the new vice principal had the right heart and was more than up to the task, the principal, by his nature, made everyone tense. He all but forbade anyone from having a good time by his very presence. During the tenure of this principal, people went to official school parties out of obligation, and the only dancers were the ticking hands of the clock.

I showed up at the party a little late and was given a seat at a table of teachers I did not know well. Our campus combined middle school and high school, and all teachers came to the same year-end party. There were literally hundreds of teachers spread out at tables of six in a large hotel conference room. I took my seat and felt the atmosphere: tepid.

Suddenly I felt a strong inspiration to go outside for a minute. As I left the conference room, I felt inspired to allow Isness to take over and see what would happen. I set Richard aside and felt a lightness envelop my energy field and body. I went back in and sat down with my group.

Within a minute or two the party was getting started. We were going to play a trivia game wherein the table that could answer the most questions won. The prize was that someone from the winning table would have to take the stage and sing karaoke. Logic told me that we would not win because I could not speak very good Japanese, and I was never any good at trivia, either — I was dead weight. Isness, on the other hand, made it clear that our table would win and that I would be performing on stage. I surrendered to this idea should things pan out that way.

The game began, and our table quickly took the lead and held it strongly. While the other teachers at my table answered questions unfailingly, I considered which song should be sung. As the final question was answered by our table's resident trivia genius, all the teachers at my table, as if they had planned it, looked at me and asked if I would like to sing. Of course, all of them were able to answer at least one question and I had yet to put anything into the process, so I suppose it was only fair. Anyway, seeing as this experience was Isness inspired, I agreed and took the stage. With mic in hand, I requested, the Beatles — "Twist and Shout."

Normally I would have been extremely self-conscious, but not this time. My body was twisting and shouting just as wildly as the song was meant to be performed. The house was on its feet as the inspiration spread around the room, and the ice melted. People were dancing and singing along with me, and even the principal was caught up in the fun. It was an out-and-out miracle as far as I could see.

The song came to an end, but the party was just warming up. The music teacher got on stage following me and dizzied up a great song. The teachers sang and danced and drank and socialized and forgot their worries. Truly it was an amazing night to head them into several weeks of winter vacation.

Unfortunately I didn't find out about it until several weeks later, when some of my friends at school asked me where I had gone after my song. You see, just as the song ended, Richard was back, and he was embarrassed. He left the stage in a state of panic, failing to notice all the teachers gesturing for high-fives as he walked back to his table. He sat down awkwardly and within a few minutes got up and left the party.

An individual who is still too tightly bound up in the self is unable to touch in with Isness easily. If they do successfully set aside the self and allow Isness to express, they may find themselves utterly stunned at the result. The more we start to release the limiting self content and tune to consciousness, the more we are able to enjoy the fruits of the process. In my case, on that night, everyone got to enjoy the fruit except me. Such a shame, isn't it?

When we begin deeply tuning to the frequencies of consciousness, the self-conscious, analytical, overbearing mind rests, and life becomes inspiring and infectious. We begin to know things that "can't be known" and do things that "can't be done" and best of all is that we are not egoistically connected to this knowing or doing. We, like everyone else, just have a ticket to the greatest show on Earth — Isness in expression.

When you can, set aside the self and allow inspiration to take over. Don't worry, the self will be there waiting for you if you want to suit it back up again. Allow the blessings to flow. And when you come back to the self, take a deep breath, relax, and allow yourself to enjoy it too.

Appreciate Beauty

During my vision quest, thanks to nearly three days of limited visibility caused by constant drizzle, I made a resolution to myself to notice the simple beauty of daily life and to appreciate everything more fully. I noticed when I went back to Tokyo, a city with some of the most incredible sunsets you will see, that people, without exception, would walk at a breakneck pace, eyes glued to the concrete, stress written all over their faces. In the midst of heavenly glory, they would walk by without so much as a glance to the horizon. In their rush to live their lives, they were missing life.

For a person on the path of unfoldment, it's vital to slow down the pace and relax into an appreciation for all that is. Be careful about turning beauty into a mental picture as that pulls us back into mind. What do I mean by a mental picture? When you look at a sunset, for example, turn off the mental words that describe it. Open up all of your senses and place the horizon in the center of your vision without limiting your awareness to it. Take it all in purely and relax into it. Absorb it deeply and share the feeling of deep appreciation for the totality. In this way, you remain conscious throughout the process instead of going into mind. Looking at a sunset then becomes inspirience instead of experience.

Taking it a step further, loosen your definitions of beauty and start to observe the whole with unconditioned appreciation, taking in the things that others might dismiss as commonplace and not worth noticing. In this manner, more and more, we can find beauty and inspirience through the senses almost anywhere. Even in the busiest most crowded places in Tokyo, it was easy for me to have sensory inspirience simply by changing my attitude toward everything.

The truth about beauty is that it comes from consciousness, not the mind. When we look at beauty through the mind, the mind begins to dissect it, to analyze it, and — worse still — to acclimate to it. You could have the most beautiful woman in the world at your side, but sooner or later she will be just normal to you if you are looking at her only through the mind. The mind will find a way to sap the magic out of everything if you feed it.

Relationship With Nature

Jon Young, naturalist and survival instructor, asserts that nature is a nutrient. This statement is a very true one. There is something that the body gets just from being in nature and absorbing the atmosphere or presence. Nature tends to be tuned to calm awareness, and by being in nature, so long as we are open to it, we quite naturally begin to tune to calm awareness as well. For this reason, having regular access to a natural environment is exceedingly helpful in the process of unfoldment.

I highly recommend that individuals take survival and nature awareness classes from instructors who have learned to live in harmony with Earth. Many schools out there support the mindset of humanity versus nature. These schools are not teaching in a way that will directly assist in the unfoldment process because their methods and intentions are based upon opposition. Instead seek out instructors who teach the approach of blending and attuning with nature. These methods will help to get us out of opposition, fear, and dominance and into the Garden of Eden.

When I took my first survival class, something amazing occurred after about the fourth day there. I noticed that my dreams changed quite dramatically. Whereas my dreams would normally have taken place in the backdrops of buildings with squares, angles, and edges dominating, they changed to being set in nature with flowing, smooth transitions and circular shapes. It wasn't just that the visuals changed; the feeling in my body also changed, and I felt as if my sleep was more productive. The first few days, before this began happening, I had poor sleep because I was not used to camping in tents. As with anything, there is a transition phase.

Remember, nature is everywhere, not just the great forests, grasslands, and deserts of the world. There is nature in the city and in your backyard. Most importantly, the closest physical thing to us, the body, is nature. Learn to be quietly aware of your body, feeling into its processes. Allow it to calm and teach you. "Or do you not know that your body is the temple of the Holy Spirit who is in you" is a very wise saying of Paul in the *New Testament*. Learn from your temple, and treat the temple with great respect. The body is not you, nor is it your prison, but it is your place of realization. Love and respect it as such, and it will teach you more than you could ever imagine. Even more than that, love and respect nature as such, and all of life will open to you.

~Chapter 17~
Caring for the Physical Body

The Amazon vision indicated that the three pillars of humanity will soon collapse, and there will be a Hell on Earth. I no longer hold any belief or opinion on if or when this will happen as neither belief nor opinion will assist in defusing (or diffusing) such a possibility, as both are of the mind and not consciousness. Instead, I tune to unconditioned love and allow that to express into the world. In this chapter I will be discussing ways to care for the body, and it just so happens that the things written here both assist in unfoldment and help us to survive during times of hardship.

There is a lot of confusion over how to take care of the physical body, and this confusion has led to stumbling blocks in the unfoldment process for many. If we can address these issues early in the unfoldment process, we will save ourselves a lot of grief and let ourselves serve whenever the need arises, as the body will be as ready as possible.

What is the physical body? A lot of people think that their body is themselves, but if we take a look at what makes up the body, we find it is more like an ecosystem filled with a great variety of living entities, all of which are made up of earth. If we were to count up all of the bacteria in our body, we would find that there are more bacteria than there are human cells. The bacteria alone in a healthy body number about 100 trillion, the vast majority of which provide beneficial services. When we add to that total the estimated cells with human DNA, another 50 trillion to 100 trillion cells, we have somewhere between 150 trillion and 200 trillion cells in the body. If our body is made up of more foreign cells than cells with human DNA, then it is quite difficult to call it us, isn't it? Each of these bacteria has requirements to survive, a purpose, and a mind of its own, just as does each human cell. What we call the body is just the sum total of all the varying cells that make it up, which changes constantly, much like the great jungles of the earth. So, just as the mind is made up of countless identifications, the body is also made up of countless individual identities.

The body functions like an energy transference system, just like the rest of nature does. Consider that the body is constructed of all of the elements that we feed it. So, are the elements that we are feeding sufficient to meet all the needs of a healthy ecosystem? If our food is being farmed, does the soil have all of the necessary elements to constitute healthy produce that our body can then consume? If our soils are highly depleted of minerals due to overuse, then those vegetables are not getting the elements that they need in sufficient quantities, and, therefore, neither are the cells in our bodies, right? If the cells in our bodies are not getting what they need, then they will not be able to provide all of the services that they are purposed for, and the health of the body wanes. Thus, if we are going to have a healthy body, then we also need to have healthy soils, too. We cannot properly take care of our body yet not take care of the earth's ecosystems, which provide the elements and services that our bodies need to be healthy. To be healthy we must realize that just as consciousness is connected to everything, so is the body.

Considering that the body is an ecosystem made up of a huge variety of different organisms, all with their own needs, we need to be aware that the body also has a mind of its own, which is designed to represent the needs of the organisms that make it up. Although the physical body is not us, it does obey us mostly. Sometimes it rebels or breaks down. Let's say that you are the general of the body, which is an army. A good general listens to his commanding officers and makes decisions according to the information that he receives from those officers. He also observes the overall condition of the service personnel when making plans. If we are wise generals and we respect and lead the body properly, it will accomplish a great deal for us and teach us more than we can imagine.

Exercise

The human body at its current stage of development functions as a hunter-gatherer collective, and it needs to be moving around every day as if it were hunting and gathering. Walking is one of the very best things for the body. All other bodily systems are toned by walking, and if we are not getting enough exercise, no matter how healthfully we eat, the body is not going to digest and use that fuel nearly as well as it would were it well exercised. The body would be healthier if it were exercised well but had a generally poor diet than it would be if it had a perfect diet but just lounged around all the time. The reason for this is that exercise tones the digestive system, allowing it to absorb nutrients and separate out toxins much more efficiently than it would otherwise. The body needs to be walking about five miles each day. But instead of walking we usually drive or go nowhere at all. I see people get in the car to visit a neighbor!

There are many possible exercises beneficial to the body, but yoga, tai chi, and other internal martial arts systems, dancing, hiking, and swimming are probably some of the best choices. Some of these exercises do very little for the cardiovascular system, however, because the movements are done slowly, so you may want to consider adding fast walking or other cardio-building routines. If at all possible, try to find an exercise that you enjoy doing, because that will keep you motivated. If you are exercising out of a sense of obligation or duty, it's less likely that it will become a regular structure in your life.

I practice swordsmanship, as well as my own energy-balancing methodology called *shinkai-ho*. These work very well for keeping my body lean and functional. I also chop lots of wood for heating the house and take regular walks in the forest with my dogs and goat to gather wild edibles and medicinals. I enjoy all of these activities tremendously, and therefore there is no negativity tainting the exercise.

If you practice the meditation as I have outlined in Part 2 of the book, as well as Dance of the Self, you may be surprised to find at some point that you can do almost any activity and enjoy it thoroughly because your enjoyment is unconditioned, and therefore the specific activity is not a factor in your enjoyment. In many cases as we unfold, inspiration may guide us to very specific activities, which is a real blessing. In any case, if there is negativity or lack of joy, then that is a perfect signal that we are tuned to mind and not consciousness.

The basic idea is to keep the body flowing with some sort of healthy movement. We want a strong, yet stable and flexible body that holds up well in extremes of heat and cold as well as dry or moist weather. We need a toned and balanced immune system, so our bodies are ready to serve whenever Isness indicates. If our bodies are out of balance, we will be unable to serve when the need is there. Because much of unfoldment happens through service, having a disharmonious body can be quite limiting.

If the body is frail because of accident or disease, then we do all we can to keep it as strong and flexible as possible while working on positive attitudes without identifying ourselves with frailty. Individuals who have been crippled by accident or disease are often able to serve in ways that those with a healthy body are unable to, so there is a natural balance if the attitudes are clear.

Trust the Body

Allow your body to choose your food. We have a free-range goat named Hana at our training facility. It's so interesting to watch what she eats day to day as she wanders around. Her diet is changing constantly with the exception of oak leaves, which she will eat year-round. One day she won't touch a certain flower, and the next she craves it. She is extremely healthy because of her natural diet.

I have often heard it said that goats will eat anything, but this is not exactly true. A goat that has been removed from its natural diet options will eat almost anything because it's deprived. A goat that regularly has choices is actually very choosy about what it eats. Just as a goat that is deprived eats things it might not otherwise have an interest in, so our bodies also get out of balance and then desire strange things.

The physical body has its own needs, and if it's in balance, it will make better nutritional choices than we could make for it. Try this game: get into a good meditation and then turn the reins over to your body. Allow your body to do the food choosing when in the kitchen. Completely forget what you like and just let your eyes go where they want to go, then pick up any food items that the body chooses, but don't consume it yet.

Before you eat any of it look at each item. Let's say that your body picks up a bag of mixed berry oatmeal. Instead of just eating the oatmeal, ask the body what it is in the oatmeal it wants. The body will pick out what it's actually interested in. You might find that your body just wanted the cranberries but nothing else in the oatmeal. Then let it eat some cranberries. With each item, question the body to see what it's really after, making no assumptions. You will find that your body is likely picking out things that you would never have chosen had you picked your food normally. Your body knows which nutrients it needs, and it will choose accordingly, but if you have food addictions, they can throw off the process. Liberation means having no addictions of any kind.

I recommend doing this activity regularly to allow the body access to nutrients and energies that it needs, but do not get compulsive about it. Many times someone else may be preparing food for us, and we should not expect that they are going to know or abide by your body's desire because that is quite a burden. Eat what is offered with joy, but as a snack fill in the nutritional gaps by allowing the body to choose.

Structuring Food

On the path of unfoldment we want as healthy a food relationship as possible. All life-forms are like rivers of flowing atoms. There are the tributaries of inhalation and absorption through the skin, but the main atomic river is digestion. Atoms flow out through exhalation, and through the skin by way of sweat, but the primary outlets are from the bowels and the bladder. Consider that atoms we consume today may have gone through countless other bodies, stretching back over millions of years. What we are eating now in the form of a sandwich may have been in a dinosaur millions of years ago! There are atoms in your food today that may have passed through the bodies of Jesus or Gautama or any number of other inspirational individuals who have walked the earth. Just as we should leave a place better than when we entered it, atoms leaving our bodies should be in a better energetic state than when they entered. This is not only great for the atoms but also the entire planetary system. Better still, it's also good for our bodies' health.

The way to improve the energetic state of these atoms starts with the frequencies that we are tuned to when eating, which has a lot to do with the degree of our presence. Have you noticed how once you start on that bag of chips it's really hard to stop? This is an example of eating unconsciously, which is to say we are not consciously present and aware of the eating process. Of course, many of the processed foods we eat have been formulated to get us to eat unconsciously by making the food addictive, but ultimately we are responsible for what we put in our mouths, right? When we eat unconsciously, we reinforcing a very unhealthy pattern. In order to turn this pattern around I would like to suggest some helpful guidelines to curb the tendency to eat unconsciously.

Consider making a personal rule of not eating or drinking while walking or standing. This is a cultural rule in Japan, one I did not appreciate at first, but the longer I lived there, the more I began to realize its value. When we are walking and eating, it's generally because we are in a rush, which of course means we are not tuned to appreciation. Another common cause is that we just do not realize that spending time with food is important, which may mean that unconsciously we believe that eating is a waste of time. If you start observing people who are walking and eating, almost without exception you will find that they are consuming sugary drinks and/or junk-food. If you have a tendency to walk and eat, consider taking a look at the structure of your life to see whether you have actually made sufficient time to sit down and eat a healthy meal consciously.

Make access to food difficult. I have noticed that a lot of people will sit at their desk and work while having their desk drawers filled with snacks. Those snacks invariably end up unconsciously popping themselves into the mouth as we work, don't they? Instead of keeping snacks in the desk drawers, consider putting them in a place that is a little difficult to get to, such as in a cabinet drawer that will require getting up from the chair. This will make us conscious of the process of eating those snacks. When getting up for a snack, take only a small amount, so we have to get up again if we want more. This will stop a lot of unconscious eating at work.

A common scenario at home is to sit down and turn on the TV with a bag of chips at the ready, which we munch on unconsciously. Consider pouring the chips into a small bowl to take with you and leave the bag in the kitchen. In this way, we can eat those chips, but if we want more, we have to actually get up to get them. Again, we are likely to eat much less in this way, and what we do eat we have to actually consider before eating.

Although the advice given on not walking and eating applies very well to a civilized lifestyle, it does not apply well to hunter-

gatherers, who often gather and eat as they walk. Of course, they are much more aware of their surroundings and are not tuned to haste or caught in distraction by watching a TV, so walking and eating works well for them. Our goat also walks and eats, but again, she digests extremely well because she is very attentive to the eating process, even while she walks. In the event of widespread collapse, we may find that we will do the same thing. This is totally appropriate in a hunter-gatherer context.

When I was a young man, an acupuncturist told me that my nervous system was overly amped up. He told me that I need to slow down my movement and to eat more slowly, to chew my food much more. He went so far as to say that I should chew each bite 100 times. That seemed pretty excessive to me, but I tried it anyway. If you've never tried this yourself, I highly recommend it. You will quickly see how habitual the chewing process is and how quickly you forget your count and start to swallow at 20 or 30. It's about as powerful an urge as when we have to urinate badly and approach the toilet to find suddenly, the urge amplifies dramatically. The body has been trained to swallow at a certain point, and it will do so on autopilot unless we become consciously aware of the chewing process.

What I noticed after retraining my body to chew more was that not only did my digestion improve, but my body relaxed much more, and my mind stopped racing so much. I used to hate massages before this change because they hurt so much, but after slowing down the eating process, massages became pleasurable because my nerves were not so hyped up. Play with your chewing count, and see what happens.

When we find that we are getting overly picky about tastes, consider fasting until the food attitudes change. Consider eating only when unconditionally appreciative of food and when there is a need. Avoid idle eating and eating while having a negative feeling, which is to say, resolve the negativity before eating. Avoid ordering food unless there is a plan to eat all of it then or later.

As you can see, a lot of eating is done unconsciously, and when we drink or eat while walking, standing, working, or watching TV, etc., almost without exception that consumption is unconscious. Consider how many fewer calories we would be taking in if we stopped eating unconsciously. More importantly, consider how much more we will enjoy the process of eating if we make the space for each meal consciously.

Food Bias

In wealthy countries there are a lot of negative food attitudes. The stress that we create in our bodies and the disharmonious energy that we put into food because of these attitudes is often worse for our bodies than the denatured food itself, so look deeply into food attitudes. If you find that you have to eat something less than ideal, then eat it with love. If you can choose a healthy alternative, then by all means do so, but whatever you do, do it with appreciation and love because some life-form ultimately constituted the matter for the food and also because that food will be going into your own body. Do we really want to add disharmony to the food we are going to eat?

An old friend of mine served in the peace corps and was stationed in a subsistence tribal area of Africa. Her group was sent there to teach them how to improve their diets. She told me how that tribe's main caloric intake was raw blood drained from live oxen. She and her companions taught the tribe that their diet was unhealthy and that they need to eat more vegetables to avoid diseases which come from malnutrition. Of course, the natives had to be taught how to farm vegetables, and the land there is not very suitable to farming.

My friend said that the natives were resistant to these changes and she could not understand why. I asked her what they looked like. She said, generally speaking, they were all very tall, lean, and muscular. I asked how their teeth were, and she said they were straight and white. I asked about the whites of their eyes and she said they were clear. I had to laugh because she is short, her teeth are crooked and her eyes are an off-white.

I asked her, "What is it that their oxen are eating?" She said, "Grass." I replied, "I think I understand why the natives were so resistant to your ideas. Oxen have four stomachs and are able to squeeze every last drop of nutrition out of a blade of grass. Oxen can digest the protein of plants, something which humans cannot do. Drinking their blood gives immediate nutritional access to all that grassy goodness. There are more nutrients in beef blood than we could ever get from eating vegetables. I am not surprised that those natives resisted what you were teaching. They look at you, and they see comparatively unhealthy, weak bodies. They see all the work you are telling them to do in order to downgrade their diet and they wonder, 'What is wrong with these people? Are they crazy?' Considering all that they put up with in this situation, it's amazing that they didn't tell you to leave."

This type of situation is common throughout the world, and its origins are arrogance, ignorance, and sometimes corporate greed. Not everything that we do is better. Later, I discovered that African farmers are being pressured to use Genetically Modified Organisms (GMO). Might there be corporate and government-level motives for "helping"? That said, my friend believed she was doing the right thing when she was in Africa, but after our conversation, she was no longer so confident.

Learn not to take food for granted, because it might not always be so readily available. Wealthy countries around the world may soon find themselves in a state of great food shortage. In that case, we will be very thankful for developing appreciative and highly flexible palates with the ability to go without for long periods of time, still remaining in appreciation.

Once, I found a couple of grubs while out in my garden. I took them up to the house, put them in a pan with a little olive oil and fried them. My wife entered the room and without seeing what I was cooking, she said, "Mmm. That smells good!" I asked her what she thought it smelled like. "Fried chicken," she replied. I showed her the fried grubs, and she was aghast. They tasted better than they smelled, I can assure you!

Most of us would grimace at the thought of eating insects, but about two thirds of the human population includes insects in its diet. They are about the healthiest thing one can eat, so long as they are not toxic. We may find them to be a ready source of nutrition when other sources are scarce. Consider acclimating to this food source.

Wild Edibles

Get acquainted with the wild edible plants in your area and start incorporating them into your diet, little by little, through salads and soups. Wild edibles are great sources of vitamins, minerals, and phytochemicals that you would otherwise have trouble getting in sufficient quantities of through even the best of modern diets. Just remember that anyone can have food allergies, so try things a little at a time to make sure your body handles them well.

I first began eating wild edibles after taking survival courses. The number of wild edibles right outside my door in Tokyo surprised me! I found the young leaves of dandelion to be a fantastic addition to salads. The entire plant is edible and extremely healthy for the body. There was also plantain (the herb, not the fruit tree), which grows almost everywhere I have ever been. It makes a great boiled green that you might prepare like spinach. It actually tastes a lot like spinach but is even more nutrient rich. Those are two great plants to start with that almost everyone will find in their lawn, but make sure you are not gathering from a lawn that you have been using poisons on.

Before gathering and eating anything, be sure to get a good plant identification guide and learn to identify plants thoroughly. Also, be sure to pick plants from non-polluted areas. There are a lot of places in cities where herbicides are used, so beware. Roadsides are not a good place to gather from because of herbicides, brake dust, and oil runoff. Even though there is a bit of a learning curve to gathering and eating wild edibles, it's well worth the time and energy. I cannot tell you how fulfilling it is to be able to step into any environment and find something to eat. What will happen is you will learn two or three easy plants and go out in search of them, and, before you know it, you'll have collected a number of other interesting plants that caught your curiosity. You bring them home and look them up, and now you have four or five plants that you know. And those four or five plants will beckon to you every time you walk past them and thereby introduce you to still more plants that catch your eye. Before you know it, you have relationships with dozens of plants, who welcome you into nature everywhere you go.

Contextual Balance

To have a healthy body, you should adjust your diet to your local environment to become contextually balanced for carbohydrates, fats, proteins, and fiber. By contextual, I mean that the percentages of each nutrient will vary according to your environment and your individual body. When living in a very warm place, the body may need a lot more vegetables and fruits than if in an extremely cold environment, where the body would need much more fat and protein.

The important thing is to eat what is naturally and locally available, as that food is balanced for the particulars of that environment. If you are self-identified as a vegan, vegetarian, or fruitarian, imagine taking a few weeks to go camping in the far north, where it's extremely cold. You will quickly realize that the body cannot survive naturally on those diets in the cold. The body will simply not be able to produce the necessary heat. For years, I was a self-identified vegetarian, and what I found was that I could not handle the subzero temperatures, for no matter how much clothing I put on or how much I ate, my body would not produce the heat necessary to keep me warm. Unfoldment is not limited to the temperate and equatorial regions of the planet, is it? Of course not. Which means that eating animal products is not a limiting factor with regard to unfoldment.

Remember, if locally available, that we can get a lot of good protein from nuts and beans, which are also excellent sources of fiber, an all-too-often overlooked part of our diet. Fiber helps to balance out our digestion process in that it keeps any nutrient from becoming too highly concentrated in the system — especially important with regard to sugar, as well as cleaning out the bowels and providing substance to our stool. Try to get as many natural colors into your foods as well. Here are just a few examples of colors that we may want to include in our diets. There are numerous vegetables for each color, so enjoy getting as many as you can, because each has unique qualities that benefit the body:

Yellow (squashes, bell peppers, corn, grapefruit)
Orange (bell peppers, pumpkin, carrots, oranges, sweet potatoes)
Green (spinach, kale, broccoli, asparagus, green beans)
Red (radishes, red tomatoes, red peppers, watermelon, guava)
Blue/Purple/Black (blueberries, blackberries, plums, cabbage, eggplant)
White (turnips, cauliflower, daikon radish, leeks, garlic)

Finally, give the body access to a large variety of fermented foods. Fermented foods provide the body with a great variety of healthy bacteria for the digestive process. If we look at any ancient or primitive human culture, we quickly see that a great portion of their caloric intake came from fermented foods, because that is one of the very best ways to preserve vegetables and beans for long periods of time without refrigeration. Not only was fermentation a practical way of preserving foods longer, it also provided the people with an extremely healthy food source that was rich in vitamin B, which the bacteria produced in the fermentation process, as well as digestion-enhancing probiotic bacteria. Modern diets are severely lacking thanks to the loss of probiotics that come from fermented foods such as kombucha, sauerkraut, kimchi, natto, miso, pickles, kefir, and live culture yogurts.

If we are getting regular exercise, eating consciously, limiting sugar and salt, and if we are careful to have a contextually balanced diet for vegetables, carbohydrates, proteins, fats, and fiber that regularly includes all colors and a variety of ferments, while allowing the body a little time to do its own food choosing, then we are heading in the right direction, so long as it's all motivated by love and appreciation.

Hydration

When I was a boy, a friend, Jeff, visited late one summer evening on his motorcycle and invited my brother and me to go camping by a stream, many miles from our house. It was a spur-of-the-moment idea, so we really had not prepared properly. It was already getting late in the evening, so walking there was not an option. Our only means of transportation at that time was Jeff's motorcycle, which all three of us would have to pile on.

Because there was no storage space on the motorcycle, we had to keep our supplies to a minimum. We brought sleeping bags, one strapped on each fender and another carried by my brother, who was in back. We taped a flashlight on the handlebars, and we were off. We rode out to the stream and set up camp, then we headed to the nearest store several miles away to get some snacks and drinks.

We messed around on the motorcycle for hours and hiked in the hills before returning to camp for sleep. Being kids, as we were, we didn't think about keeping hydrated. I probably went to sleep mildly dehydrated, but after a few hours of sleep in the dry air combined with the mosquitoes pulling every last bit of blood from my face that they could, I awoke in severe dehydration.

I have been through a lot of pain in my active life, but nothing compares to the overwhelming pain that comes with severe dehydration. I awoke unable to move, think, or speak. I knew I needed water, and that was all I knew. I tried to move, but my body would not respond. I tried to scream, but all that came out was a moan.

I don't know how it happened, but Jeff must have heard my weak moans. He came over and asked me what was wrong, I tried to say water, but it came out more like, "Waaar."

I repeated it a few times, and he asked, "Do you need water?" Not waiting for my answer, he lifted my head to a cup of water. I somehow managed to drink it down, and before long I was back to myself again. It's a scary thought, but I was probably not too far off from unconsciousness, which would probably have resulted in death. To me it's a miracle that Jeff woke up because of my weak moans. But thankfully he did.

Transpiration is probably what took most of the water out of me. Many of us are familiar with perspiration, which is when the body releases water through the pores onto the skin, which slowly evaporates and cools the surface of the body. Transpiration is the same except the water evaporates immediately and, therefore, we do not realize that we are sweating. When the air is extremely dry, transpiration is what is happening, and it's a silent killer. When in arid climates we have to drink regularly, even if we do not feel thirsty, because the body is constantly losing water through transpiration, and we can find ourselves in severe dehydration in a snap.

Extremely humid environments are also dangerous because it's extraordinarily easy to suffer heat stroke as the sweat remains on our skin, failing to evaporate in air that is already saturated. In such a case, the body is not cooled through perspiration, yet it's still sweating. We need to keep up with our hydration while also being careful not to overheat.

All of us have experienced minor dehydration, which we would feel first as thirst, but relatively few of us have experienced severe dehydration, thankfully. I don't recommend it. Severe dehydration can kill quickly and painfully, but minor dehydration also exacts a toll on the body and the mind.

Even in the case of minor dehydration, the body loses strength, flexibility, and reaction time. The brain no longer functions as effectively, leaving us in a mental fog. Many people confuse the feeling of dehydration with being hungry, and they eat. Doing so exacerbates dehydration as the body uses water to digest. When thirsty, avoid any caloric intake, which is just one of many reasons drinking any sort of sweetened, caloried liquid is ill-advised.

So what are the progressive symptoms of dehydration? When the body is properly hydrated, it is at optimal physical and mental performance and is able to regulate heat normally. At the onset of thirst, the body has lost about 1% of its water, which causes slight performance decline and altered heat regulation during exercise. At about 2% water loss, thirst is further increased while heat regulation and performance is further hindered. The decrease in performance is between 20-30% when water loss is at 4%. At 5% water loss, headaches, fatigue, irritability, and feeling "spaced-out" are common. At 6% water loss the body's ability to regulate heat is greatly compromised, and one experiences obvious weakness. When the body has lost 7% of its water, collapse is likely if exercise is not discontinued. By the time the body has lost 10% of its water, it is likely comatose. Beyond 10% loss of water, death is likely.

[Nutrition for Cyclists, Grandjean & Ruud, Clinics in Sports Med. Vol 13(1);235-246. Jan 1994]

Overhydrating can be dangerous, too. Surprisingly, long distance runners have died from drinking too much water, which hyper-increases blood volume, diluting salt (electrolyte) concentrations in the blood. This causes saline levels to be lower in the blood than in cells, so through osmosis, water starts to move into the cells, oversaturating them, which can lead to breathing disorders, headaches, and even death if the brain cells swell too much. The increase of blood volume in the circulatory system stresses the heart and kidneys, leading to damage of kidney cells.

Some symptoms of overhydration (water intoxication) are as follows: fatigue, headaches, confusion, nausea, vomiting, irritability, restlessness, cramps or muscles spasms, seizures, unconsciousness, coma, and, sometimes, death.

As with all things, we are looking for a balance between the elements of the body. Those individuals who consume less salt and eat more vegetables, which contain water, do not need to drink as much to maintain a balanced water/saline ratio in their blood. Individuals who consume a lot of salt need to consume more water to balance saline levels in their bodies. The climate, with regard to heat and humidity, and physical activity are huge factors in the salt-to-water ratios, too, so how do we figure out how much to drink?

The basic rule is to have constant access to water, which we sip little by little as we feel thirst. If we observe that the mouth is not dry and there is no thirst, then we hold off drinking. A lot of people have learned to ignore their sense of thirst, which causes hydration issues. With regard to overdrinking, which can easily occur during times of high physical activity, consume no more than seven ounces, which is about seven normal swallows, of water in a 15-minute period to avoid overhydration. The body is telling us through thirst when to drink and when not to, if we only listen, but when drinking, do not guzzle. We can look upon this as another opportunity to observe.

Biorhythm

One very common challenge for people in modern culture is maintaining a healthy biorhythm, which is the rhythm of bodily processes. People often lack a consistent schedule for both eating and sleeping. This causes the body not to digest or sleep well.

When I first moved to Japan, I suffered horribly from lack of a stable biorhythm. I had three different part-time jobs, so each day my schedule differed tremendously. On Monday morning, I had to be at work early, so I got up at 6 a.m., but on Tuesday I didn't have work until 1 p.m., so I slept in. The schedule differed every day! What I found was that after a few months of doing this, I simply could not sleep, or I would wake up at odd hours if I did. Even if I did sleep, my body never felt well rested. Eventually it got so bad that I was in a constant mental fog, and I fell into depression. I had very little stress tolerance, so I got upset easily during this time, and my body was hyper-reactive to stimulus as the nervous system was stressed to the maximum. My body felt hard and brittle at this time.

Fortunately, for me, I lost all my part-time jobs in the very same month when those businesses closed their doors permanently. It was just a month before the regular school year began, so I applied for a junior high school job, which I got. This regular job gave me a fixed schedule that had me out the door by 6:50 a.m. every day. My sleeping pattern improved tremendously from the regular wake-up time, as did my digestion thanks to eating at regular intervals.

The biggest challenge for people with regard to biorhythm is finding a reason to get up and move out every day at the same time. Even those of us who have regular jobs tend to sleep in on the weekends to make up for the exhausting week. This is not a good idea. Get up at the same time, even on weekends, but take it easy during the day to recover. In this way, the body's rhythm will not be disturbed.

There are a lot of health problems that actually come from having insufficient sleep and a mixed-up biorhythm. For a person on the path of unfoldment, being mentally fogged, exhausted, or overly nervous will make the meditation process quite challenging, so addressing biorhythm issues early on is well advised.

One of the best ways to correct biorhythm issues is to get up at the same time every day, regardless of what is happening, and not take naps during the correction process. This can be a real challenge for individuals who are already sleep deprived, but if you allow yourself to sleep during the day, then the rhythm never can correct. Stay up until that time when you would ideally go to sleep, and then go to bed, and no matter how poorly you sleep that night, get up at a decided-upon time and stay up. The biorhythm will correct itself in short order if this is done faithfully.

If you find that you awaken in the middle of the night and have trouble getting back to sleep, it may be what you are consuming before sleep that is causing the restlessness. Consumption of alcoholic drinks, certain medications, caffeine, or high concentrations of sugars in the evening can disrupt the sleep cycle in the night and bump us out of sleep.

If we are not sleeping deeply and sufficiently, then we will feel dull in the morning, and this will affect our levels of awareness throughout our day. Be aware that the body is very sensitive to light and the seasons, as well as to where we live on the planet. All of these factors regulate sleep. During the summer months, it is natural to require less sleep due to greater light stimulation than in the winter months when daylight is shorter and the body needs more sleep.

The maxim of getting seven to eight hours of sleep a night is probably insufficient for meditators, especially in the early stages. Allow your body to get good, long, deep sleep if at all possible, and allow the body to acclimate to the natural light cycle. There are no night people when electricity is no longer available. People, even those who claim they are "night people" will end up going to sleep much earlier when natural light is the only source available. The high-intensity light from bulbs and computers is what allows for the "night person." So, turn off all sources of unnatural light early if you want the biorhythm to correct. After doing so you should find that you awake at or just before sunrise, refreshed and ready for a good, productive day.

Bodywork

During the active process of unfoldment, there will be times when the body binds up with disharmony as stresses of life reflect deeper issues within. During such times, it's extremely beneficial to have access to a good, energetically aware, body worker who can get the body flowing again. In Japan, before any meditation session with Sensei we would practice *shinkai-ho* therapy to open up the body's flow. After doing this the mind would clear, and then tuning to higher frequencies and remaining tuned to them became exceedingly easy.

Of course, we were still not very grounded in the tuning process, so we used *shinkai-ho* to leapfrog us into consciousness. Ultimately we do not want to become reliant on bodywork for the tuning process, but bodywork is important to care for the body and keep it flowing so that it does not rebel or fail us by making our path of unfoldment unnecessarily difficult.

I continue to regularly do *shinkai-ho*, which is sort of similar to a totally formless and inspired yoga, I suppose. The body moves entirely on its own during this time, so there are no forms or planned movements. Reaching the point when movement begins to occur spontaneously is vital to the process of unfoldment, because this is when the spirit is doing the work, and the mind and the self are no longer being fed.

Still, it takes a great deal of time before this process will become active in an initiate's body. Usually, I can pass this on to students directly through repeated touch that awakens the body, but most individuals will not have access to such direct experience with me, so we will need to find other means through which we can open up the body.

I found that energetic massage therapy can be very beneficial for individuals who are physically bound. I can imagine that there are numerous therapy types that would work well for such situations, so long as the practitioner is energetically sensitive. For practitioners of bodywork, you will find the meditations that I teach will bring your energetic work to extremely powerful levels if you practice them regularly.

Every day, spend a little time after waking lightly stretching to get the body flowing. We can do this through a light intent on opening the body in all directions. Do not focus on any one point, but instead relax into the frequencies of consciousness. Keep the breath smooth and easy, but do not use breathing techniques. The body knows how to breathe properly for any situation if we are calm and not feeding identifications.

The teachings of non-concentration, non-will, and non-method are probably quite distinct from most approaches. Just try it out, and I believe you will find that you are able to open up the body without injury or willfulness. Use the intention of unfoldment and the principles of meditation to enlighten your movement. In this way, you will make rapid progress.

~Chapter 18~
Caring for the Mind

Through most of the process of unfoldment, there will be a great percentage of time spent unconsciously tuned to the frequencies of mind as we release and resolve identifications, little by little. Within the frequency classes of mind there are very low-frequency emotions such as hate or depression and low frequencies of thought such as "I am a loser" or "Nobody likes me." These low frequencies have no direct benefits to the body, which is to say that they are purely disharmonious. But in the higher frequencies of emotion, such as personal love or self-confidence, and in the higher frequencies of thought such as "I am happy" or "I am loved" we are tuned to the mind; we would at least like to be in the higher frequencies of mind as much as possible, so that making the leap to consciousness is not such a challenge. For this reason, we must address certain seeds of darkness that are truly burdensome to the process of tuning to consciousness.

Loosen Expectation

Expectation is defined by the Merriam-Webster Online Dictionary as "a belief that something will happen or is likely to happen." What this definition lacks is the other half of the picture, which is the emotional rebellion that occurs when expectations are not met. To expect is to sow the seed of disharmony.

Imagine: it's Monday morning and time to leave for work. You get in your car and turn the ignition. The starter clicks a few times, but the engine doesn't turn over. You turn the key multiple times, first praying that it will start, but soon those prayers turn to curses under your breath. You have a dead ignition, and now you are going to be late for work. Of course, you expect that your car will start, so you have an emotional reaction. We understand that the function of a car ignition is to start the car, and, of course, we gain value from that function, but at some point that ignition may fail. Having the ability to understand a function and to be able to anticipate that function allows a person to be able to make plans, but when our emotional stability is built into those plans, that is where the seed of rebellion is planted. It's the emotional tie to expectation that is the cause of the reaction. Ultimately we want to be free of the tie, as well as of the emotional reaction, so that expectation no longer binds us.

> The Master can keep giving because there is no end to her wealth.
> She acts without expectation, succeeds without taking credit,
> and doesn't think that she is better than anyone else.
>
> — *Tao Te Ching*

Lao-Tzu here describes the life of an individual who is tuned to the Tao, not the individual who is tuned to egoic desire. Many of the structures and relationships of our lives are heavily impregnated with expectation. We want to slowly and surely defuse the power of expectation from these structures and relationships. In order to do so, we relax into an aware flow without going into willfulness.

Notice the emotional reactions that occur every time expectation is not met. For some individuals reaction to expectation is obvious, and for others it's barely noticeable, but do not compare reactions. Any disharmony, no matter how small, is still disharmony, so we observe and resolve it.

Notice how we use emotional force to push people to do things that we expect of them. Notice that they may do as we expect, but the services rendered are steeped in obligation and disharmony. Currently our entire economy is run by expectation, which causes tremendous stress on the entire planet. Humankind is so steeped in this expectation that we do not know there is another possibility.

Because expectation is of the mind, there is no way out of it so long as we are tuned to the mind. Therefore we begin to tune to consciousness, and, little by little, we relax into the flow without expectation. The transition should not be willful, so we will ease our way toward less expectation, less anxiety, which means less disharmony, all the while acquainting ourselves with unconditionality.

Life without expectation is not a life of nonproductivity. What will happen is that the more we are tuned to consciousness, the more inspiration there will be. Inspiration will become the primary motivation, not expectation. When this begins to happen, our lives become much more positive.

Start to map out how and when expectation pulls you out of the present, turning you into a machine of obligation, anxiety, and stress. Correcting other people is the tendency, but this is not really helpful, so make it a priority to observe and resolve your own habitual disharmony instead.

Maintain Integrity

He who is faithful in what is least is faithful also in much;
and he who is unjust in what is least is unjust also in much.

— Luke, The New Testament

Your word is your oath, and nothing more need be added to it, otherwise it loses power, and you bind Soul. If you agree to do something, then in order to maintain integrity and not bind Soul, you must fulfill your word. Of course, if you gave your word in the past, and now your conscience speaks against it, then apologize for not fulfilling your word, for to act against conscience is ill-advised at any time.

Such a simple teaching but so difficult to master, it seems. The vast majority of people speak from the tip of the tongue, so what they say is not what they do. They make promises lightly and do not follow through. For a person walking the path of unfoldment, this habit is highly detrimental. A great deal of unfoldment, once one is past the initial phases, occurs through service; if one is not trustworthy, then what service is there? We can meditate all we want, but if there is no trustworthiness or follow-through, then there can be no true service. At some point, we will hit a wall that will halt our progress because our motivation is selfish and our word is weak. Then we will wonder why we aren't respected, why we are aimless.

Whenever committing to something, observe the mind. You may find that it isn't harmony doing the talking. Better yet, observe the mind whenever talking, and do not allow for too much idle talk. Through idle talk, we bind Soul tremendously.

A good exercise, once we are ready, is to carry around a pocket notebook and a pencil. Keep a record of every time you say you are going to do something. Write down exactly what you have committed yourself to, and date it. At the end of every week, look over those notes and check the commitments that you have completely fulfilled. Doing this exercise will help make us aware of idle commitments and spur us to keep our word.

Beware of Painting

As a child, despite my generally quiet nature, I loved nothing more than to play tricks on people for fun. One Christmas I was gifted a two-foot, ribbed, plastic tube that mimicked the sounds of an Aboriginal bullroarer — a string with a wooden instrument at the end that makes a special sound which travels for miles when swung around.

I found that I could produce myriad strange sounds by blowing through this tube. One Sunday afternoon, while playing with it, I found that I could make quite believable animal sounds — especially the singing, whining, and howling sounds of coyotes, which were numerous in our area. While I was practicing coyote vocalizations outside, I noticed one of my neighborhood friends riding her horse up a trail in the hills behind my house. I decided to see if I could convince her that there was a coyote in the bushes on the hillside.

I quickly climbed the hill where she was heading and positioned myself out of sight, behind a large tumbleweed. As she drew nearer, I began my calls. I started out somewhat erratically, sounding as if a pack of coyotes had just made a kill. I suppose she didn't really understand what my calls meant anyway, so I could do any coyote sound I wanted and she would not know the difference.

When she first heard the sound she was obviously quite interested in checking it out. She turned her horse to bear down on the sound and approached slowly. As she got closer I was worried that she would be able to see me, and the joke would be spoiled, so I started making growling and yipping sounds intending to put a little fear into her. Luckily she responded exactly as I had hoped; she stopped her horse immediately. Her stopping told me that she was worried that there might be a danger, and being the fun-loving boy that I was, I reveled in her fear. I intensified the growls and yips even more, well beyond what any wild coyote would conceivably do. To my surprise, she whipped the horse around and galloped away, downhill, into the neighborhood.

I was pretty satisfied with the convincing sounds that my new instrument could make, but a little disappointed that the fun was over so quickly. I decided that I would have to find a new victim, and quickly. I was having too much fun to stop with just one scared girl. So I decided to come down the hill and see what she would do after she calmed down, all the while keeping my eyes open for new prospects.

To my surprise, she didn't do at all what I expected. I thought that she was going to tie up her horse and go into her house to tell the story to her father, which would get me into trouble if I were caught. He wouldn't be too happy about me scaring his daughter while she was riding her horse, a potentially dangerous situation. I certainly didn't want any angry parents on my hands, so I quickly abandoned the location where I was hiding and stashed my toy until I was sure the coast was clear. Fortunately, instead of going to her home, she went to mine instead. I had to assume that it meant her father was not home, so she decided to go next door, to my house, to tell her story.

This got me thinking. Knowing my brother and sister, they would be way too curious to let an adventure like searching for some coyotes pass them up, and if I were right, I could expect them to be coming up my way in very short order. I decided that I had better get back to my previous hiding place and wait for the posse.

And what a posse it was. Clearly, my brother and sister called some of the other kids in the neighborhood, as there was a little horde of people: Natalie, the horse rider; my brother and sister; and two other kids from next door, as well. This was getting good.

They were coming up the opposite side of the hill that Natalie had been on earlier, which was good for me, as there was more underbrush for me to put between the posse and myself.

I started making coyote sounds when they were just halfway up the hill, which turned their dead-run into a freeze session. After a few expletives they started out again, but this time at a slower pace. The trail they were using was quite narrow thanks to the thick sagebrush and tumbleweeds, so that they had to come up single file, which limited everyone's view except for the leader's.

The kids in back were excited and obviously hungry for information. They kept up a constant barrage of questions to the leader, who did a look-turn-answer all the way up the trail. Their progress was slow, and from what my ears could gather, the leader, my brother, loved all the attention he was getting. He had them believing that he could see a coyote and its pups well before they were even 50 yards from me.

Being on a hillside made their voices echo pretty clearly, and I could catch a lot of what they were saying. Of course, my brother couldn't actually see anything except for the bushes between us, but he certainly was convincing. By this time, my adrenaline was pumping pretty hard. I knew if they discovered that I was playing a prank on them, they would beat me to snot. My brother wasn't one to be made a fool of, and the people who would typically have protected me from a beating were unfortunately also looking pretty foolish at this point. I couldn't count on their protection this time around. I had only two options: to try to sneak away unseen, which was going to require a miracle, considering how close they were to me at that point; or to put on such an impressive sound show that fear would prevent them from coming closer and discovering it was me and not a coyote. I chose option number two. Not only was it safer than sneaking away, it was by far more interesting. I figured that if I got caught, at least I could have a good laugh before my beating, and if I survived, it would make a great story.

I started snarling with more intensity as they came closer. I also made some whimpering sounds as if there were puppies present. I figured that my brother would know enough about coyotes to realize that they do not normally make noise in this type of situation unless they were backed into a corner, injured, or protecting pups. Of the three, a mother with pups is always the most dangerous.

Once my brother heard the whimpering, he started pointing to the bush I was behind and saying he could see the mother and pups. Soon the others came up next to him and started leaning forward to peer toward the bush. I was wearing blue jeans and a white T-shirt with white sneakers. I knew at this range that they could probably see me, and that if I didn't turn them on their heels immediately I would be caught.

I deepened the growling sound to an ominous level. It didn't stop them from coming up any further. By this point, they were within about 10 yards of me, and I tried not to look in their direction for fear that they would see the whites of my eyes — always a dead giveaway.

At this point, my brother was counting the pups and saying that he could see the legs and tail of the mother, which had a gray coat. I was beside myself as my fear took a sudden detour into humor. I had to use all my willpower to repress the giggles that were bubbling under the surface, threatening to burst into howling laughter.

They got within five yards or so, judging by sound, before the reality of my precarious situation hammered humor back into fear. I broke into a panic-fueled primal growl and began shaking the bush. It was so intense that it would have caused anyone to fear for his or her life. I wasn't acting anymore — I was panicked.

My brother froze. Silence. This was the deciding moment. I knew his fear was overriding his curiosity. I poured on the violence. He made his choice, a blind-panicked, run-for-life retreat.

I peered over the bushes to see if they were far enough away for me to make my own escape. I knew it wouldn't be long before my father came up the hill to check out the situation.

The posse was heading toward my house, and I wanted to beat them there. I ran straight down the hill, where no trails existed, crashing recklessly through the dense underbrush. I was determined to beat them to the house, even though I knew I was risking injury, as there were many holes and large rocks that I couldn't see under the brush. I wasn't worried about the racket I was creating, as they were making so much noise that I was sure that they wouldn't hear anything above their own terrified screams.

I reached the bottom of the hill, ran straight for our backyard fence, and quickly scaled it. Fortunately for me, my mother had been doing laundry earlier, so the back utility room door was unlocked, which was not usually the case. I ran through the utility room, into my bedroom, locked the door and shut the drapes.

My clothes reeked so badly of sagebrush that I tore them off and stuffed them in my closet. I doused myself with some cologne, which I was also given for Christmas, and quickly put on new clothes. This whole process took less than a few minutes, from the top of the hill to new outfit.

There was still no sign of the posse, but I knew they would be showing up soon, so in order to look completely oblivious to what was going on I made like I was busy doing my chores. I ran down to the barn, which I usually did at that age — running everywhere, I mean, and fed the cats, while singing out, "Here kitty, kitty, kitty," which brought in hordes of cats for food every time. I could hear my brother coming up behind me, and I suddenly felt a wash of self-consciousness. I was certain that he must have suspected something. Surely, someone must have seen me. Or maybe I had some unchecked cockleburs in my hair. That would be a dead giveaway.

To my surprise, he came into the cat room and started blabbering on incoherently about some crazed coyote and pups on the hill, and how I missed it all. My self-consciousness turned to a strange sort of objectivity bordering on the scientific. I pretended as if I were completely in the dark about this whole coyote business and started asking him questions about it to see if he really believed his own story.

To my amazement, he seemed to believe wholeheartedly that he had seen the mother and pups. He told me she was wounded and that he was sure she would have attacked if they had taken one step closer. I was having trouble accepting that he really believed his own story. My curiosity kicked in, driving me into potentially dangerous territory. In order for me to test his conviction, I would have to tell him the truth — that it was I on the hill, making the entire ruckus. It was the only way I would know if he really believed his story or not.

I told him everything, in detail, even going so far as to reproducing the sounds. He told me that I didn't sound anything like what he heard on the hill and that I was full of crap. He swore emphatically that he saw everything with his own eyes and that there was no way that it could have been me.

Baffled by his hard stance, I showed him my concealed, sagebrush-smelling blue jeans and T-shirt and pointed out the location where I played the coyote on the hillside. He still didn't believe me. And to my greater surprise, he wasn't the least bit angry with me. If anything, he seemed somewhat bewildered.

Before I knew it, my sister walked into the house and started blathering on about the coyote to my parents. Bewilderment turned again to conviction as my brother chimed in with full force, wanting to outdo my sister with tales of his bravery and leadership and how he saw everything while the others had merely gotten a glimpse of the coyotes.

So I pushed even further and told my story to my parents. Nobody believed me. This was one of my first experiences with how the mind can play tricks on us. Sometimes, we want to believe something so badly that our minds actually fill all the holes and paint in the elements that we need to reinforce our beliefs. I have always held that experience close to my heart, and I have been as careful as possible not to jump to conclusions or "paint" experiences.

Unless a person is aware of this painting tendency of the mind through actual experience, much like I had, painting is likely to be a common way of interpreting reality. And for one walking the path of conscious unfoldment, this kind of painting can be extremely disadvantageous. We must strive to remain as calm and centered as possible when we experience things and not get caught up in emotional fervor, which gives rise to the artist within.

Be Your Own Devil's Advocate

A thousand years ago people believed that the world was flat, a notion we now know is not true, but were you to go back a thousand years ago and speak to anyone on the planet at that time, most would think you were nuts if you asserted that the world was actually spheroid. Looking at science a hundred years ago and comparing those ideas to contemporary science, we find that much of what they thought then to be true does not hold much water now. How much of what we believe to be true now will hold water a hundred years from now?

Just as the popular beliefs and "facts" of a thousand or a hundred years ago no longer hold much water, the beliefs and ideas that we personally hold onto may also be incomplete. Instead of trying to justify and protect our ideas, we might reverse the process, and try to prove them wrong. In this way, not only will we no longer be feeding the ego, but we are also likely to find any weaknesses in our perspective, which will eventually cause us to look much deeper than we might have otherwise.

Once, when I first introduced students to a spot of dark energy in the room, something strange happened that really spooked everyone. The students filed out of the room, through the hallway, and into the main room, but just after the first person went past a partially open door without touching it, the door opened for the second student by itself.

Everyone saw the door move, and frankly it was quite startling. One individual said it was a spirit that opened the door. I asked each student what they thought happened, and the common view was that maybe it was a ghost or a spirit. I said, "That could be, but now it's our job to look into it deeper and test that idea."

We all went back into the room and restored the door to the very same position it was in before we filed out the first time. Then, in the same order, we left the room, careful to walk at the same speed. Sure enough, just as the first person passed the door, it moved again. We put it back and walked through once more. Again the door moved. What we found was that the door was so light and hung in such a balanced way that the slightest breeze would cause it to move. The cause was not a spirit; instead, it was just a draft of air that was moving the door.

When training with my teacher in Japan, we would intentionally try to counter each other's techniques. It was due to this disproving that we were able to go beyond technique to something more profound and irrefutable. Had we continued practicing purely in a cooperative fashion, then this deeper level, which is consciousness, would not have been found.

The basic idea is that no matter what you believe or what you practice, try to prove it wrong or find a weakness in the method. But don't just test once. Keep at it over and over, from differing angles and perspectives. Otherwise you can easily overlook something valuable by way of assumption. Be the devil's advocate for yourself, because if you have not found the holes, then as you go further down the path of unfoldment, the devil surely will.

This approach will turn off a lot of people who are likely to become frustrated when you punch holes in their theories, ideas, and methods, so do not be rude or egoic about being the devil's advocate, as that will only kick up identifications. Instead of directing this approach at other people's ideas, direct it at your own beliefs.

This simple change of intent will goad you deeper and deeper until you find the root of ignorance and resolve it to Isness. Any time you find yourself protecting a certain position or building up a belief system, do what you can to disprove it. When you have stripped away all, and nothing remains but pure being, which really is no-thing, then you will have found perfection.

When we consider the incredible amount of strife in the world over belief systems, methods, and cultures, we can see that if all people were to embrace this one simple approach, those divisions would disappear as each nation resolved to Isness. Of course, we cannot expect that other people will do this. Instead, we always begin within ourselves and allow that to project into the world through the radiance of consciousness.

Starting with ourselves may seem like the slowest way, but actually it's the fastest. The ego will always tell us that we need to promote this idea or that idea to change other people's minds. But the war of ideas and the desire to change minds is itself of the mind, and, therefore, we remain stuck in the matrix of mind that is disharmony. Instead, take the seemingly slow route by tuning to consciousness and questioning your own mind. Be your own devil's advocate, and disprove your mind time and again until you lose faith in the mind. In this way, consciousness will be revealed through you, which will light a spark for all who are ready to take the same step.

Soften Memory Identification

While I lived in Japan, I worked as a middle-school teacher. I had a homeroom class and a group of students whom I taught intimately through their middle-school lives. They felt to me in some ways as if they were my own children.

Toward the end of my career at that school, numerous factors brought me to stress levels that were too much for the body to handle. Probably the most important factor was the vision that I'd had in the Amazon and the trauma that I held onto after being shown the probable futures of collapse that humanity was unconsciously moving toward. Add to them the great earthquake and tsunami that hit the country in March of 2011, knocking out electricity and causing a nuclear plant in Fukushima to go into meltdown. The entire country was thrown off kilter. We were rationing electricity and wondering whether life in Japan would ever be the same. The economic stresses of the world had been hitting the country hard as well, so there were some harsh policy changes at our school that had divided the teachers, creating animosities. I didn't have the stability to move gracefully through those circumstances.

One morning after midterms, I went to my desk and sat down to grade tests. I began with my homeroom class, picking up the stack of tests, unfolding them, and turning to student number one. *Strange*, I thought, *who is Ai Wada?* This was not one of my students. I flipped to the next student and again could not recognize the name. I rechecked the class, and indeed it was 3A, which was my homeroom class .... Someone must be playing a joke on me, I thought. Then I got out my grading book, which was locked in my desk, to verify the names. I flipped to 3A, student number one and it was Ai Wada. I knew that my grading book was unmolested because it was in my own handwriting, and, therefore, the data there must be correct.

Ai Wada was my student, and she had been my student for years. I had helped to raise her through her junior high experience, and suddenly I could not recognize her. I had forgotten her. How terrible. What's more, I had forgotten all of my students, whom I loved very much. "What is wrong with me," I thought. "Do I not love my students enough to remember their names?" Then it occurred to me that I had forgotten almost everything. I knew my name, but I could not remember the names of other teachers, apart from a few old friends at the school.

Tears began uncontrollably pouring down my cheeks, and my body began shaking. I was in a terrified panic. Another teacher came over to talk to me. I turned my head away so as not to reveal my shame. He didn't realize that I was having an emotional breakdown right in front of him, and he walked off, seemingly offended that he was ignored. I got up and walked out of the school, telling no one. I remembered how to get home, and so that is where I went. My wife called the school and let them know that I would be taking sick leave for the remainder of the week. I spent the next few days in a depression, not remembering enough to be able to do anything useful. I called my father by phone and told him what had happened. He said that he'd had the same experience many years earlier, and that it was a temporary memory loss due to too much stress. He assured me that the memories would come back soon, and that I should just take it easy and rest for a few more days.

The next day, I had an unexpected insight. I realized that, although I couldn't remember anything, I was still me. My existence was not dependent upon memory. And as soon as I realized that, the depression was gone. Of course, without memory, certain functionality was missing, but I was still me, which meant that I could still be happy, regardless of the loss of memory. I began to enjoy my days off, and in short order memory returned.

Memory, which is in the ninth spectrum of disharmony thanks to our identification with it, is a necessary tool to function in daily life, but it can also be a curse when we identify with our memory. The fact is that memory is not a stable thing. Once we understand that memory is a biased recording of events that is constantly being rewritten in our minds every time we tap it, and that the data there corrupts with time, then we can appreciate how unstable it really is. Memory is not actuality. Memory is not even the past. Memory is similar to imagination in that it's quite mutable. For this reason, we cannot use memory as a way of being present. Memory is never present, and its accuracy degrades over time. Of course, we should appreciate the functionality that memory allows, but we need not attach our sense of self to "our past."

One interesting exercise is to play with the idea that you have no memory at all, apart from essentials. Forget things like your favorite food, what you like to do, or where you like to go, and then just change up what you eat, what you do, or where you go for a day. Try something new, or do something old but in a new way, but don't be foolish about it.

Many of the most healthy attitude changes occurred in my middle-school students when we were on school trips. They just needed to get out of their usual rut in order to step into a new perspective. Do not seek to be comfortable during this type of exercise. Just soften your pattern to the point at which you are willing to try something new with an open mind.

Identification with memory can be quite the prison, limiting your perspective greatly. Take a holiday from memory, and enjoy a new perspective. Often we cannot embrace new perspectives or step out of old patterns while maintaining our usual life situation, with its ruts and habits.

Beware of Positionality

The questions "Who am I?" and "What am I?" are ones that philosophers and laymen alike have been asking since humans have had the ability to speak the words. This question stems from Soul, so anyone on the path of spiritual unfoldment will eventually ask it. Of course, the question as it typically comes through the mind is so pointed and biased that it makes having insight difficult.

On occasion, throughout my childhood, I would go outside on clear starry nights, lie down on the lawn, and gaze up into the vastness of the universe. Because I lived in a small rural town, there were few lights to interfere with the cosmic beauty of space. Sometimes the skies were so clear and the stars so distinct that it felt like you could just reach up and pluck one from its dark nest in the heavens.

I would relax so much into the gazing that it began to feel as if I no longer had a body, as if I was the cosmos. But if I did not have a body, then what was I, I wondered. Curiosity began to move me into a search for self. If I was not my body, then was I thought? But then, I had moments wherein there was no thought at all, and during thoughtlessness, I still was, so I could not be thought. Was I emotion? No, because during the time of thoughtlessness there was also no emotion. Was I memory? When gazing at these stars I was so relaxed that memory was not even present, so I was not memory. "What am I?" I wondered. All I could say at that time was that a very clear sense of "me-ness" existed without any further defining attributes.

Little did I know at the time that those experiences were profound moments of insight into actuality. Of course, I would come out of me-ness and pop right back into Richard, who was a body, thought, emotion, and memory. Still, unbeknownst to me at that time, a seed was planted that began to grow.

As an adult I had unexpected insight into the unconscious identification process while watching the movie *Avatar* at the cinema in 3-D. I remember being drawn into the movie so deeply that, at some point, I was no longer Richard; instead, I was one of the tall, lean, blue, Na'vi natives in the forest. I snapped out of it and realized what had happened. I had unconsciously identified myself as an alien from a distant planet.

It sounds ridiculous, doesn't it? If we watch our children, they identify with characters on TV all the time, getting so entirely engrossed in the process of identification that they make games of it. Adults, for the most part, might not get so deeply engrossed as children do because much of their identification is already tightly defined, but we do identify ourselves unconsciously with thoughts, emotions, opinions, places, and things almost constantly. And when someone challenges those things, well, we may not like that so much. Such challenges cause the frequent violence that occurs during sporting events. Whether adult or child, the automatic identification process is so smooth and habitual that it's happening nearly constantly, without our noticing it, through association.

A nice game to play is the game of nonpositionality. In this game, we lovingly allow space for everyone's opinions. We have no stake in opinions and positions during this game, and instead are interested just in allowing for communication. Spend the entire day not defending any thought, emotion, opinion, position, and so forth.

Consider all things to be equally possible, as if we lived in a fantasy world. Allow people to express their ideas fully and question those ideas to draw them out even further. Do not confront their ideas, even if they seem really illogical. When questioning an idea, do it with love, and be careful not to shut the idea down.

Do not be spineless or wishy-washy. You may still suggest an idea, but take no emotional stake in "your ideas" or "facts." Do not make yourself "right" and the other person "wrong." If the person likes your idea and accepts it, then fine. If they ask for clarification, then clarify if you like, but if they argue against it, do not defend anything. Instead, flow with them to see where they are heading. They are free to accept your idea or reject it, just as you are free to accept or reject their idea; moreover, you are free to accept or reject the idea that you thought you supported originally.

After this exercise, you may find that your perspective on things has changed. It's not that anyone changed you, or even that you changed your perspective willfully, but more like your perspective just opened up and began to flow. Do not concern yourself with whether the other individual changed or learned anything. That is not the goal. The goal is to soften the self content and "our" positions.

Embrace Structural Change

One of the biggest and most frightening challenges that one faces in the process of unfoldment is structural. I am referring here to the structures of your life. Your relationships, job, social standing, your home, comfort zones, habits, addictions, interests, entertainment sources, opinions, likes, dislikes, diet, language (including body language), movement of the body, and so on begin to change to match the shifts that are occurring in your perception as Soul unbinds, your mind silences, and you begin to see things more clearly.

It's not that there is some outside source telling you who you need to hang out with or what you need to eat, but instead, it's the flow of your very being that is inspiring you in new directions. In many cases, your family, friends, coworkers, etc., who may not be spiritually unfolding at the same rate that you are or who may have no interest in unfoldment at all, might try to hold you to their expectations of who you are to them. As you change there may be resistance from those who are frustrated that you are not the same person they thought you to be. Some may even outright try to prevent you from "changing" because they want you to be the person that they know you as. Many may simply not find you interesting anymore and move out of your presence. If we are worried about other people's opinions of us, then that is just another level of binding that will prevent us from realizing oneness. Liberation is not for the weak or cowardly. It takes great courage to face all of the fear and illusion that we hold on to. Embrace courage, and let it flow through observation.

Remember to do the Dance of the Self often so that when these changes occur you are not imbalanced too much by them. Allow things to happen at a smooth, even rate, and enjoy the process; it's not a race. The people who no longer jibe with your energy field will eventually distance themselves, and new people who are more in accord with your field will gradually be magnetized to you. The process will take time, and there may be a long period wherein you feel as if you have no one with whom you can speak of spiritual matters, but that will pass eventually. Joining a meditation group for companionship through this process may be a good idea for some.

Notice Idol Worship

The greatest idol-worship is not the worship of objects but the worship of the self. Worship is not just when our hands are clasped in prayer or when in fellowship; we worship with our attention primarily. How much of our attention is on the self? That is how much we are worshipping the self. The only time we are not worshipping the self to some degree either directly or indirectly is when our attention is on silent, unconditioned love and ultimately Isness.

Personality worship is just an extension of idol-worship. *Person* is a word that is derived from *persona*, which in Latin originally referred to the masks used in theater. The persona is a mask that the individual has created over many lifetimes to protect the self and/or to gain a social advantage. The person is just a mask, no matter how much we believe it to be us. Do not confuse the personality with the actual individual. Neither Soul nor the Spirit is the personality.

Even among people who are not consciously unfolding, this confusion about personality often creates misjudgments about the individual. I have noticed that on first introductions people tend to be attracted to extroverted, sparkling personalities, and that less glittery individuals get overlooked or underrated. But when we watch relationships over the long-term, often those sparkling personalities fall short. Frequently they suffer from critical issues like lack of follow-through, untrustworthiness, selfishness, etc., that they use personality to insulate. Those who are far down the path of unfoldment very rarely have flashy personalities.

> "The Master views the parts with compassion,
> because he understands the whole.
> His constant practice is humility.
> He doesn't glitter like a jewel
> but lets himself be shaped by the Tao,
> as rugged and common as stone."
>
> — *Tao Te Ching*

We will find that as our energy is removed from the person and directed to Isness, we will become less interested in flashy people. In all likelihood, we will seem somewhat dull to ordinary people but captivating to those who are consciously unfolding. So the question, then, is, whom do we want to attract? Once we have insight into the personality, then we understand the motives of the self and others, and we are no longer misled by glitter.

Belief Systems

Sometimes people will join my meditation group and get upset because these teachings appear to conflict with a pre-existing perspective or belief system. The conflict comes when the individual holds a belief system to cover for a sense of insecurity and/or a sense of hopelessness. When we look into any belief system, what we find is that the self gains some sort of hope through the belief system. It gives the self a feeling of having a concrete foundation to hold on to, right?

But the self itself is an illusion, a mental construct. The self is the first belief system. And it's because the self is inherently insecure that it needs to construct overlaying belief systems to try to patch security holes. Just as there is always a weakness to any patch, though, there is always a weakness to any belief system. So long as there is a self, there is a belief system, even if we have not recognized it. The end of belief systems does not come from no longer believing in them, but instead from the deep realization that the self itself is an illusion, a belief system. Some would call what I am saying, "killing the self" or "the death of the self," but how can something that never actually existed be killed? How can an illusion die? We are not killing the self; we are just seeing through it, which is to say, we are opening to the infinite.

I know that many self-described atheists and agnostics would claim that they do not have belief systems, but actually they do because they believe in the self, even if unwittingly. They also tend to believe in physicality, in the senses, in the mind, and/or in science. Even science can be a belief system because it's based on the mind. Mathematics, for example, is the attempt to measure what is inherently immeasurable. Mathematics creates an artificial construct to encapsulate what is actually infinite. We can best see this in the calculation for the area of a circle, which uses pi. The number 3.14 represents pi, but in actuality pi is a far longer number than 3.14. In fact, there is no end to this number. Pi's first 30 digits are 314159265358979323846264338327, but the number actually stretches on into infinity. The benefit of using 3.14 to represent pi is that it gives us a functional enough circle to work with. The benefit of mathematics is that it allows for a practical construct for the mind to function within the universe to a degree, but the disadvantage is that if we attach ourselves to it, there is a barrier that does not allow for the realization of the infinite. If we were able to completely remove all emotional ties to mathematics and view it only as a tool of the mind for functional purposes, then that would not be a binding belief system. In this way, we can still make use of mathematics as a tool, if we wish, without binding to it, which allows us to be more open to the infinite and the undefined.

Because all beliefs represent the self content, I encourage students, little by little, to untie from belief systems. It may not be possible to fully untie instantly because, for a lot of us, belief systems are compensating for traumas and deep-seated insecurities. Thus, to give up all belief systems immediately would feel extremely threatening to the self and would create defensiveness, avoidance, or even aggression. Therefore, we release little by little as we gain trust in the infinite and undefined. Once we realize the degree of flowing stability and strength that comes from being free of belief systems and ultimately the self, then it's very easy to take that final step into the infinite. Until then we take it very slowly and carefully.

Paradoxically, when all has been released and the infinite shines through, there are hope and belief, but hope and belief of this type are not of the self. They innately come from the infinite and, therefore, they are unconditioned, which is to say they have no mental construct or emotional tie. To have unconditioned hope and belief, we remove all conditions of the mind through tuning to the frequencies of consciousness. Then we find, counterintuitively, that there is clarity and hope by default without any ascertainable cause. These qualities have power so long as they remain unconditioned.

True freedom largely means freedom from belief systems through unbinding. Such unbinding and embracing of the infinite are at the core of what I teach, for truly there is no way to teach what Isness is because it's formless and free of all definition. Therefore, the only belief that matters is the one that is blocking us from resolving to Isness. "Empty your cup," as the old Chinese saying goes — but do it gently and carefully, starting with what we are ready to release. To release more than we are ready to causes willfulness, and that does not aid in this process.

The Danger of Teachings

I have had several students confide in me that they used to buy every spiritual book that they could get their hands on. They would play spiritual audiotapes when driving, recite mantras and affirmations. For all of it, they found themselves with more mental noise than they had before reading any spiritual books. When trying to meditate, their minds would repeat wise sayings and insights to them. The teachings had become millstones around their necks. One student took all his books outdoors and burned them, so frustrated was he. He decided not to read any more spiritual books because he was so fed up with the noise.

You see, the mind will feed on any information that you give it, and it can turn any great teaching into disharmony. "Do not give what is holy to the dogs; nor cast your pearls before swine, lest they trample them under their feet, and turn and tear you in pieces" (Matthew 7:6). If we consider that the dogs and swine in this statement represent the mind, then this teaching helps us to understand the dangers of the mind and what the mind will do to spiritual teachings.

There is a true danger that comes with any teaching. The danger is that the individual receives the teaching through the mind. Whatever the teaching is, if it's received through the mind, that teaching will become just another set of trivia in the mind to think about and debate. This thinking and debating is all from the mind, and it feeds identifications, which ultimately bind Soul even further.

Therefore, true teachings can be either binding or enlightening, depending upon which route they are taking, the mind or consciousness. Jiddu Krishnamurti, in his book *Total Freedom*, has audiences with various scholars who end up debating with him in frustration. This is the inevitable consequence of teachings being received through the mind. Had those individuals listened through consciousness they would have seen clearly, with insight, what Krishnamurti was saying, and there would be no need for debate. But because they were working through the mind, each little point was resisted and debated, creating more disharmony than before they had spoken with Krishnamurti.

If we receive his teachings through the mind, we suffer from thinking or create a belief system, both of which are of the mind and disharmony. But if we go deeply into the higher frequencies of harmony and receive the very same statements from Krishnamurti, we will find that we understand much of it clearly — it's obvious. There can be no debate when two people have insight into something, because both will have the same fundamental insight. The reason is that insight comes from one source, Isness.

Tune to consciousness, and many spiritual teachings become simple and obvious, assuming they were passed on through consciousness. Unfortunately, there really are a lot of teachings, the majority probably, that have come to us through the minds of the teachers and dogmas of traditions. Such traditions are not transformative. They sound wonderful, and the mind tends to crave them because the mind can feed on them, but they do not resolve the self. The only way to realize the difference between accurate teachings and inaccurate teachings is through Isness.

If we are tuned to consciousness, then we no longer feel the need to burn our books. Instead, we can enjoy reading them and feeling the degree of accuracy of each book. Through reading while tuned to consciousness we can gain a lot of great insights from almost any book, really, possibly beyond what the author was intending to teach.

Wanting Needs

The vision quest was an extremely valuable experience for me in so many ways, but one of the biggest things I got from that time alone in the forest was the realization of really how little I actually needed to be happy, and also how owning lots of things becomes a burden as the things in our possession actually own us. I reflected on my life and realized all that was really necessary for me was to have a shelter, food, water, love, and an inspired purpose. I realized that most of my wants were actually attempts to fill an empty space inside.

I began to notice how, when we buy something new, like say a car, for the first few months it feels fresh and exciting, but after a time, the mind begins to adjust to the item, and it no longer feels special. Pretty soon we are getting hungry for a different new car. We might or might not buy that other car, but the urge for that new car experience is there, and we start comparing it to our old new car, causing it to lose esteem in our minds. This desire is an illusion that traps many of us in the never-ending hamster wheel of debt and misery. Once I was aware of this tendency of the mind, whenever that tendency arose, I could see through it. I began to be quite happy with my meager belongings. I pruned down my possessions to fit into 10 or fewer cardboard moving boxes, so that I could just load them into my car and move with ease as I was pulled here or there by Isness to study.

Since that downsizing I've met a number of wealthy individuals who, despite their holdings, have little or no ease of mind. They have asked me how I can be happy owning so little and having so few desires. "The answer is simple," I say. "Our desires actually represent the self content. If we have a lot of wants, it's only because there is disharmony within." Once we understand the tendency of the mind is to try to patch over insecurity and instability with desires, then it's pretty easy to choose consciousness instead of mind and needs instead of wants. And the more that people do this with dignity, not identifying themselves as "poor," the easier it will be for other people to make the same decision."

Sense of Purpose

Many on the spiritual path struggle with finding a sense of purpose. One reason depression is so high in first-world countries is that although people are busy and work a lot, in general they do not have a sense of purpose beyond the self. For someone walking the path of unfoldment, a lack of purpose beyond the self is all the more difficult to deal with. Many get stuck at step one because they do not know what that one special purpose is, so they just wait to find out.

In a few rare cases, individuals may have a clear indication of purpose very early in life, and unfortunately the accomplishments of these individuals usually get highlighted to the exclusion of how the process normally works for most other people. Just as not everyone's true love shows up in high school, neither does our one true purpose show up easily (assuming everyone has one true purpose). In fact, for most people there may be many smaller purposes before they find a big one. Or maybe the individual is well suited to many varieties of service beyond the self. We should have no assumptions here.

Soul often speaks through passion. If we are inspired or passionate about something, so long as our conscience is in accord, then pursuing that passion will open doors for the unfoldment process. It does not matter if the passion is for something considered to be important or not. It could be something as simple as a hobby, or it could be something large like starting your own business. Once we start following our passion, that passion will lead us to the experiences that will expedite the unfoldment process.

If passion eludes, look into the health of the body as there may be some issues that are blocking passion. If passion still does not rise, then consider doing a vision quest to reveal it. If that does not help, then simply apply yourself to something beyond the self that your conscience agrees with. This will get the flow going, and through this flow of purpose, you may realize that you have found what you were looking for, or you may move from one thing to another. In any case, you have a purpose, a sense of service, and that buoys the spirit. Remember, have no expectations, but remain open to the possibilities.

Forgiveness and Reconciliation

One of the most difficult and sensitive areas of the unfoldment process deals with forgiveness and reconciliation. Forgiveness is such a misunderstood process, and thanks to this misunderstanding there is a lot of resulting disharmony and victimization in the world. First and foremost, forgiveness is not of mind, but of consciousness. The mind does not have the capacity to forgive because the mind is conditioned. Any forgiveness that the mind conjures up is a conditioned forgiveness, which is not forgiveness at all. The second misunderstanding is the belief that forgiveness and reconciliation are one and the same, though they are not. Forgiveness is something that you realize on your own through resolving negativity, by tuning to consciousness, but it's not something that we can expect of someone bound in the mind. Reconciliation, meanwhile, requires the agreement and follow-through of all parties involved. The crux of the matter is that we do not control what other people do. They are not our job. We can do only our part, which is to tune to consciousness so that negativity can resolve.

Because of the confusion between forgiveness and reconciliation, victimizers will often take advantage of the commandment to forgive by pressuring people into forgiving and then interacting with that individual again. Take an alcoholic, abusive spouse as an example. He drinks and beats his wife. The next day, when he is sober, she says she will leave him. He apologizes and cries, saying he will never do it again. The next week the same thing happens again, so his wife decides to draw the line and says she is leaving. He then says, "You're supposed to forgive me. Jesus says you must forgive, right?" The abuser guilts his wife into giving him still more chances.

If we step back and look at what is really happening, we can see that her staying with him is enabling him to continue the same negative cycle. She is willing to forgive in hopes that he will change, but he is not doing his part to reconcile, which in this case means to make the change he promised. In light of the lack of reconciliation, often the best thing she could do for herself, this individual, and her children, is to end the relationship. He is not going to change so long as he is comfortable. People do not change when things are comfortable. Only when there is some pressure, either internal or external, that creates some discomfort does a person wake up and change their ways. Of course, for the sake of Soul, forgive, which means to release any emotional negativity toward the individual. But for the sake of all involved there may need to be a hard line drawn in the sand as well.

Usually when we think of forgiveness we might imagine one person forgiving another, but that is really only a part of the picture. A great portion of forgiveness needs to happen toward ourselves. Through my unfoldment process, memories of things I said or did to myself or others that I felt bad or embarrassed about will pop up. I locate the negative feeling in the body and dance it out. In the same way, if the memory of someone else arises and there is negative feeling toward them for their actions or even just for "bad chemistry," I dance it out, which keeps things from getting intellectual.

Dance of the Self is an extremely useful tool that can be applied to a great variety of situations on the path of unfoldment, but it's a tool that we use only until we are so connected to Isness that there is no longer any need to dance out negativity because there simply is none. Isness never forgives because there is nothing to forgive, which is to say Isness always forgives instantly. When we have reached that point of grace, nothing gets stuck emotionally, yet we are still able to make clear rules and boundaries for the sake of all involved.

When I was suicidal, a voice spoke through my chest, giving me direction in life. One of the first things it said was, "Find friends who are working for something positive, who have a purpose in life that you respect." One of the best and easiest choices that we can make in life concerns who we spend time with. If we are surrounded by people who are tuned to low frequencies, our own frequency will tend to drop unless we are already far along in the unfoldment process. Thus, if we wish to tune to a higher frequency, we can choose to be around individuals who are tuned to consciousness, right? In order to do this we must begin to take command of our space. You must be the general of your space, or others will be.

Prayer

"But seek first the kingdom of God and His righteousness,
and all these things shall be added to you."

— Matthew, The New Testament

I consider prayer, as it's commonly expressed, to be a very

dangerous thing, indeed. What I have noticed is that even when people get what they want, it rarely benefits their lives, which is to say they are not happier in the long run from getting what they want. If you could choose to grant everyone's prayers just as they request, would you? Would that be healthy? How long would it take before we destroyed the planet with our prayers? Human beings are still bound in the self, and, therefore, our desires are quite dangerous.

I personally never ask anything for myself through prayer because to ask for something for myself is indicative of mind-based prayer. Oftentimes, though, prayer does come through spontaneously, and when it does it's always through the higher frequencies of consciousness, which means that it's not the mind that is directing the prayer. Instead prayer is happening of its own accord through the body. Such a prayer is truly powerful.

The danger is when we are in mind and praying, which is what is commonly occurring with people now. Such a prayer, whether we realize it or not, even if it is for other people, is inherently selfish as the mind is entirely of the self. What I would suggest is that tuning to the frequencies of consciousness is prayer — the highest and truest form of prayer. Even if we requested nothing, the frequency alone is benefiting all that is. Therefore, how could there be a better prayer? When a specific prayer needs to be stated, then it will come through us spontaneously and effortlessly if we are open to it.

Consider deritualizing, dewilling, depersonalizing prayer and, instead, allow prayer to be in its rightful place, which is Isness. Sometimes personal prayers happen through the frequencies of consciousness, so they are not of the self; instead, they come from Isness to express through the body into the world. In this case, the prayer is not from the self but from Isness.

Consider the statement of Jesus: "Most assuredly, I say to you, the Son can do nothing of Himself, but what He sees the Father do; for whatever He does, the Son also does in like manner." (John 5:19).

This statement is full of insight; what a beautiful hint of consciousness. Untrue prayer is from the self, whereas true prayer comes from Isness through the body to the world.

~Part 4~
Soul and Spirit

Have you ever wondered what the difference is between Soul and spirit? Is there a difference at all? Judging by the many religious and spiritual writings that use these words, there is little or no difference between them, as they are usually used interchangeably. Looking these words up in the Merriam-Webster Online Dictionary does little to clarify, as the meanings are nearly identical.

Soul: the immaterial essence, animating principle, or actuating cause of an individual life ... the spiritual principle embodied in human beings, all rational and spiritual beings, or the universe.

Spirit: an animating or vital principle held to give life to physical organisms ... a supernatural being or essence.

So, what is the difference between spirit and Soul? For the sake of this book, I define them distinctly so as to highlight their differing functions within the multiverse. These terms may be used differently by other teachers, but I need to differentiate these two things to clarify function and allow for a flow of understanding. Please forgive.

As was stated earlier, everything in the multiverse has Soul, including elementary particles and atoms, but only life-forms have individuated spirits. Soul is the image-free energy that is in each individual in the multiverse and beyond. Each and every atom in the multiverse has Soul. All cells and organelles within cells have Soul. Plants and animals, planets and stars have Soul. Humans also have Soul. Soul is immortal and timeless. Soul cannot be bought or sold, nor can it be killed or destroyed. Soul can be likened to water in that it is formless as a gas but mutable as a liquid. Like the way frozen water maintains the form of its container, Soul also takes on the dimensions of its container.

Soul provides the possibility of unfoldment. When Soul energy is used responsibly, in alignment with its pure nature, great love, integrity, and service are possible. Soul is not the self, although the self is constructed of Soul energy. It's only when one sees through the self that the true power of Soul can shine through unhindered.

The spirit is the body-image-template of the individual life-form within the multiverse. The spirit, like the self, is entirely made up of Soul energy. We could say that spirit and Soul gas are different phases of the same energy. When the physical body dies, the spirit initially retains some semblance of that body. If one were able to see all of one's human incarnations one would be able to see the similarity between the spirit and the physical appearance of each incarnation with regard to the image.

The self can be described as a temporary construct that serves functionality within the immediate incarnation. Because the self is meant to serve functionality in the world, it contains much more detailed information than does the spirit. The self is found entirely in physical memory. The spirit contains overarching themes such as incarnational memory, incarnational/unfoldment trajectory, virtues, vices, talents, passions, et cetera. By contrast, the self contains much more specific information that is subject to rapid change relative to the information held in the spirit. The information of the self includes your personal name, likes, dislikes, proclivities, specific knowledge, your favorite TV shows, sports teams, and so on.

In this section, we will learn of the relationship between the self, the spirit, and Soul and how that plays out in the wheel of life. From this foundation, we rediscover the true transformative power of unconditioned love, a power without which humankind would be eternally bound in the matrix of the mind, suffering from the trauma that is the birthright of a sense of separation.

~Chapter 19~
The Wheel of Life

After the physical death of the body, the individual perspective continues into a nonphysical phase that is typically called an afterlife. In truth, there is only one life, and that life is not limited to the body. The individual perspective goes into a body and expresses, and when that perspective leaves the body it goes through what can be likened to Heaven and Hell experiences. Neither of these experiences is eternal, but experiences of Heaven and Hell feel eternal.

Heaven

When a life-form dies, the individual's perspective rises from self, to spirit, and finally to undifferentiated Soul, like ice, to water, to gas. As the individual's perspective ascends metaphysically, less-empowered identifications, limited to the self, are resolved to pure Soul. As the light of Isness intensifies further, the stronger identifications, fearing exposure of their corruption, turn back, remaining in the atmosphere of the planet to survive parasitically on other creatures. These identifications, being unresolved, await the return of their Heaven-sent other parts, with which they will parasitize during the next incarnation.

Once the all negativity has been shed, the spirit goes through a phase of spirit memory projection, similar to a dream, wherein the individual vividly projects its best times in its favorite habitats surrounded by vibrant life and friends. These spirit dreams contain no negative emotion and are therefore much more vivid and meaningful than experiences of physicality, which contain negativity that disturbs the experience. With each memory sequence, the spirit becomes increasingly more transparent and brilliant, eventually leaving only Soul in formless, blissful oneness — true Heaven. Like water drops entering the ocean, the individual no longer is.

The process of Heaven gives us a great hint as to the differences between a Graduated Soul and an undergraduate. The most obvious difference between the spirit of a Graduated Soul and an undergraduate is that the spirit of the Graduated Soul exists only to serve; whereas the spirit of an undergraduate still contains parasitic identifications that do not serve. Because the Graduated Soul no longer harbors parasitic identifications, its perception no longer needs to move through phases, as does the perception of an undergraduate, although a Graduated Soul can go through phases as service requires. Whereas the constituent parts of an undergraduate are divided and often conflicting, all is unified for a Graduated Soul.

The purity of Soul shining through a fully functioning, identification-free body in service is what undergraduates are ultimately gravitating toward during incarnation. This condition is the Heaven on Earth that Jesus spoke of 2,000 years ago, when he said, "behold, the kingdom of God is in the midst of you" and "the kingdom of God is within you." We are tuning to the frequencies of consciousness to unveil this inherent purity. When functional purity becomes our reality, then we are ready to graduate.

As the time nears for the next incarnation, the individual's perspective descends into the spirit, which takes the form of its next incarnation, to become familiar with the perspective of the new life-form. It's instructed by others of that species, learning what it is to be in that form. It's a timeless, loving place in an ideal body that does not age, practicing, playing, and preparing. When the spirit has completed its preparations, it is conceived through the right genetic combination, time, and place for its incarnation so that the individual can have the experiences it needs that ultimately prepare it for eventual unfoldment.

The stages of Heaven are the same for humans as for all other life-forms, but there are certain differences in details thanks to belief systems that color the experiences as we gravitate nearer to Heaven after death. We can get a glimpse of the subjective nature of these experiences through the differing stories of heaven as represented by different cultures and religions. When Buddhists die, for example, they may have to cross a river to enter into Heaven, whereas a Christian may perceive climbing a staircase and going through a doorway or gate. It is common among many cultures to travel through a tunnel into the light. Still, many other people experience being met by family members, ancestors, or spirits who guide them into a brilliant light.

There are individuals who have died, gone to the threshold of spirit heaven briefly, and been sent back to do more work in their current incarnation. The stories often differ in the details, but the fundamentals are the same. These individuals had unfinished business and needed to go back into the body to complete that business. This type of business is always for betterment on a spiritual level. The personality that gives the message is not as important as the message itself. A Buddhist may perceive that the message comes from Buddha, whereas a Christian may speak with Jesus. One might just hear a voice in the light that may be perceived as God. Still, others are greeted by family members who give them the message. The point is not to get caught up in the personality or the images. Look deeper, for when the spirit is shed and all that is left is unconditioned Soul, these details will mean nothing.

As one's perspective nears the threshold of pure spirit phases of Heaven, one will be in the atmosphere of knowingness yet still have conditions of the self, which is to say that one feels deeply what is being experienced is absolute truth, even though it has illusory aspects. The difficulty here is that there is still sufficient connection to the conditions of self, so even though there is the feeling of knowingness until the spirit is shed, the truth perceived is conditioned to some degree. For this reason, a Buddhist, a Christian, a shaman, and an atheist could reach the edge of spirit heaven and come back with significantly differing stories.

Whatever and whomever we see in spirit heaven is a projection for the sake of communication and is not entirely real. However, these projections carry a message that helps to get the individual back on track in life according to the individual's stage of unfoldment. Forget the messenger and pay attention to the message, because back on Earth there will be conflicting accounts of other individuals' differing experiences of "Heaven." The only stage of Heaven that is not at least partially a projection, for undergraduates, is the stage of pure Soul wherein the spirit is fully shed.

Once in the pure spirit phase of Heaven, the presence of Isness is almost palpable. Undergraduates will perceive Isness through the filter of the spirit, and positive memories. Thus, a Christian may perceive Isness as a white light, for example, or an old man with a long, white beard. A Hindu may perceive Isness to be a totally formless presence, or as a favorite god such as Vishnu. In any case, it's a profoundly peaceful inspirience. The perspective then transcends the spirit, and what is left is formless, timeless, unconditioned bliss wherein there are no more projections. This is the deepest and truest state of Heaven for an undergraduate, and at this stage, all undergraduates are having the same inspirience, although they probably will not remember it because the mind is not active in true Heaven.

Once the pure Soul stage is complete, perception descends into the reforming spirit to prepare for the upcoming incarnation. During this phase, the individual may perceive being instructed by a Graduated Soul. The undergraduate is shown the degree of darkness and division that they are working toward resolving in their next incarnation. At this time the spiritual hints, the core relationships, and important events that are to be encountered during our incarnation are scripted onto the spirit. During the upcoming incarnation, these scripts attract experiences and people that serve to funnel us into unfoldment.

The pre-incarnation phase feels eternal, yet paradoxically we can still gauge time peripherally during it because of a pressure that builds around us to pull our perspective back into physicality. Regardless of the details, the feeling of Heaven is timeless, like an eternal moment of bliss. Like water evaporating, only to condense back into drops to rain down, onto the earth, and refreeze — so does the perspective of the undergraduate rise and fall.

Hell

Just as there is a Heaven, there is also a Hell. This Hell is for individuals who are so consciously identified with evil that they have effectively shut down or drowned out conscience, and it no longer speaks to them. Only unfolding individuals are able to experience Hell; flora and fauna do not have Hell experiences.

Although ordinary people may have done many things they are not proud of, things they may continue to do, each of them still has a conscience that is, at least, attempting to speak to them. These individuals sometimes lie and cheat, or they reactively think and harbor negativity, but they do not consciously identify themselves as being evil. They do not revel in malice but instead regret it to some degree, even if they are not be able to entirely stop the wrong behavior. These types of individuals are not the people who experience Hell.

Primarily, Hell encompasses individuals who are self-identified with darkness and revel in it or defend it. Let's use a murderer as an example, one who loves the feeling of power he gets from the fear in his victims, and who is a perfect example of a being self-identified with malice. Such an individual lacks the ability to enter the light of Heaven and is instead redirected to a Hell experience. What one experiences in Hell is entirely a projection of the individual's self-identified malice. Although such individuals are in quarantine and entirely alone, they do not perceive it that way. These individuals believe themselves to be surrounded by potential victims to slaughter, and they kill seemingly endlessly until they grow utterly sick of the hollowness that always arrives once the thrill of the kill fades. They begin to wonder whether there is any meaning in their lives, and whether killing will always leave them feeling hollow in the end. Once this observation sets in, they eventually reach a point at which they grow sick of killing and would rather die than to kill again. They begin to yearn for some deeper meaning in life.

At this moment the individual's Hell experience ends. The once deactivated conscience becomes active again. The individual perceives himself in a comfortable learning environment and reflects on his life with a respected teacher or mentor, whom he trusts deeply and instinctively. The individual ponders his former incarnation and finds the points at which he made choices against his conscience, and he gets the opportunity to make new choices. When all of his decisions are in alignment with conscience, his spirit rises to spirit heaven in advance of his next incarnation. He is born once more into a physical body with an active conscience, which he now values. During such incarnations the individual still has to account for all actions taken against conscience, as Hell does not absolve that responsibility. With his conscience reawakened, he can continue through the cycle of rebirth until he discovers the truth within himself and resolves all nonserving divisions.

White-collar crime, in general, is a very easy way to turn off conscience because criminality is so rarely detected or prosecuted, as compared to street crime. Because individuals can commit such crimes with ease, they commit them often and easily, thus expediting the deactivation of conscience. Another quick avenue of conscience deactivation is doing things against conscience by justifying the action as legal. Many of humankind's laws are not actually moral or ethical, and conscience will often speak against actions that those laws support. Do not be seduced by the statement, "Why not? It's perfectly legal."

Destructive addictions are also a pathway to Hell — whether a sex addiction, food addiction, drug addiction, or even a video game addiction. The type of addiction is not the main factor in determining whether the individual is Hell-bound. The determining factor is whether the addiction is central to the individual's life so that it results in near-total dysfunctionality — and whether the individual defends or even promotes the addiction. If such individuals have not resolved this problem before the body dies, they will go through a Hell experience. No matter the type of behavior, if our conscience is turned off, it leads to a Hell experience.

These severe addictions point to deeper emotional issues, ones for which addiction is a mere symptom, and so during one's incarnation, the productive thing to do is to take courage and look at whatever is causing such addictive drives. If one takes the time to observe one's mind, the cause can be found, and resolution can occur. The difficulty lies in the identification behind the issue which has convinced the individual that looking into the issue will be too painful, and that the individual is not strong enough to do so and maintain sanity. What the identification never reveals is that the addiction is already proof of a lack of sanity. Observing the issue is the only way to re-establish sanity.

When addicted persons' physical bodies die, they will have a Hell experience wherein they gorge themselves with their addiction, experiencing its destruction over and over countless times until they become so entirely sick of it that they utterly refuse to touch it again — and don't.

Hell, properly understood, is not a punishment, but is instead a time-out for the sake of the individual and society. Hell helps us to get out of a rut that has blocked all possibility for a healthy interaction with life. When conscience is turned off, spiritual unfoldment is no longer possible, and a time-out is necessary to face the issue head-on without interruption.

When the right circumstances appear for such individuals to return to the realm of experience, they are born into a family that has the right genetics for their physical body, talents, intelligence, and personality traits. These individuals are born at a time when they are able to work out relationship issues they share with others — people with whom they still have unresolved energy. Truly, every condition needed to work through in that lifetime may be met by being born into that particular family, in that particular place, at that particular time. In this way, all that the individual spirit wishes to accomplish is within possibility.

Rebirth

When the undergraduate, who was the source of the identifications that turned away from Heaven, reincarnates, identifications return in phases as the individual matures because they can eat only if the individual has the ability to respond to certain stimuli. As a baby becomes a child, a teen, a youth, a worker, a parent, middle-aged, and so on, identifications re-enter each according to the phase of human development that they are able to feed upon. Whenever identifications emerge, there is an opportunity to resolve them to Isness, should the individual have the awareness, right attitude, and understanding.

In order for an individual to graduate, all identifications must be resolved to Isness so the energy that was bound up in them can be put to use in true service. Ignorance created, sustained, nurtured, and protected identifications through a sense of otherness, and through self-protection. For this reason, we do not want to push identifications away, which would be just another action based on otherness. Unconditioned love rooted in Soul is the alchemy that allows for identification resolution.

The idea of maintaining an unconditioned, loving space that welcomes even parasitic identifications may be hard to accept, but that is the way of Heaven. It is not heaven that refuses identifications, but the fear of Heaven within identifications that causes them to turn away. What they fear is being fully exposed. Many of us will discover that we feel an urge to condemn identifications, even if we know better. Whether we admit it or not, we believe that such condemnation is an effective strategy to protect ourselves. The irony is that condemnation is itself an identification, and a powerful one at that. Once we realize fully that condemnation is an identification that we have been feeding, and also that condemnation does not bring about positive change in the world, we stop investing Soul into that strategy. Identification resolution occurs to the degree that we consciously embrace Soul.

Taking this notion further, we also learn to hold people who would call themselves our enemies, people who would do us harm had they the opportunity, in the space of unconditioned love. Once we unveil and fully put unconditioned love to work in our lives, we find that no one can harm us, no matter how they try. If they are able to harm us, that is because there is still a certain amount of condition to our intention, some disharmony or dysfunction within.

How is reincarnation a just way for life to express? Looking into it, we see that through reincarnation we create the world that we will again be born into. Considering the degree of corruption throughout society, the rate that we are overpopulating, depleting resources, polluting, and destroying ecosystems through action and inaction, what kind of world are we going to be born into in future incarnations? It's a frightening thought, isn't it? Nonetheless, an unfolding individual makes the best of whatever life brings, for to do otherwise is to feed victimization.

Because we create the world that we will be born into, it's useless to complain about our life and the world; instead, we must do something to improve that world, to reduce suffering, which ultimately means that we must resolve our own darkness and act through purity of unconditioned love to actually exert some beneficial impact.

That stated, it's not necessary to believe in reincarnation. What's important is that we tune to unconditioned love, rooted in Soul, and allow it to express into the world. In this manner, quite naturally, the world will improve through our expressions and actions of unconditioned love. Many of our beliefs are really excuses not to love; thus, we let go all beliefs and remove all excuses not to love. No matter the situation, turn to unconditioned love, rooted in pure Soul, and there can be no regrets.

~Chapter 20~
Removing the Veil

The path into the light seems dark,
the path forward seems to go back,
the direct path seems long,
true power seems weak,
true purity seems tarnished,
true steadfastness seems changeable,
true clarity seems obscure,
the greatest art seems unsophisticated,
the greatest love seems indifferent,
the greatest wisdom seems childish.

— *Tao Te Ching*

Everything within the multiverse has Soul, even atoms, because all is ultimately an expression of Isness. Just as when ignorance defines itself it produces a mental bubble, a universe, so also does the individual, when self-defining, produce a mental bubble that is fueled by Soul. As that bubble is filled with energy, it takes on a life and identity of its own, which I call an identification. All identifications are inherently unstable because there is no stable answer to the question "What am I?" The furthest one can go toward that answer and not create a disharmonious mind-bubble or identification is to say, "I am."

Identifications, both positive, such as, "I am kind" or negative, such as, "I am a loser," are disharmonious because they are not true, and consequently they are always leaking energy and need to feed in order to survive. They parasitize their creator, the individual, by agitating and causing stress.

The individual feeds identifications by reacting to the agitation, unconsciously binding a little more Soul energy into these dark bubbles. And with each reaction awareness of Soul is further veiled. I call this a bound soul. As Soul binds, the individual is pulled deeper into the matrix of the mind, a very disharmonious and insecure place where thoughts and emotions constantly harass. Therefore, bound souls have no peace until they unfold and graduate.

Identifications all exist within certain energetic frequencies, and when we live our lives tuned to those frequencies, quite naturally we are feeding and creating identifications. As a result, we suffer from the matrix of the mind. But there are still higher frequencies that do not feed or create identifications, but instead resolve them back to the pure Soul, which is harmony. By remaining in these higher frequencies the energy of Soul gradually unbinds, which ultimately leads to true liberation.

When one tunes to the lower-frequency classes — emotion, thought, memory, or imagination — Soul energy is bound. When incorrectly using the senses, which means to focus on one sense to the exclusion of others or to focus all senses on one thing to the exclusion of the totality, the sensing stimulates memory, imagination, thought, and emotion, which also bind Soul energy. But once we realize that we have a choice as to what we tune to, we may begin tuning into higher frequencies and, thus, gradually find freedom.

Whenever consciousness is used incorrectly, it binds up some Soul energy into a dark form. Just as the multiverse is the projection of self-definition, so does projection within the consciousness of an atom or an animal or a human cause Soul-binding. For the human, the birth of a thought-identification(9) begins when an individual identifies the self with a mental statement such as "I am ugly" or agrees with someone's assertion "You are ugly." At that moment a sliver of Soul energy gets bound up as the ugly id-entity, which will then assert "I am ugly" whenever it needs to feed. The individual's mental/emotional reaction is the food.

It's probably easy to see how the statement "I am ugly" would create disharmony for the individual, but what about the opposite statement: "I am pretty"? Isn't that good for the individual? No, it's not, because it's using the mind, which is based on opposites, contrasts, and comparisons. If I am pretty, does that not by definition mean that other people are uglier than me? I am holding myself up and unconsciously putting others down. What happens when someone is prettier than I am? If my sense of self is tied to my appearance, then I have been put down. It's this comparison process, a process born of a sense of otherness, that is the imbalance. Whenever we play this game, we sliver off a little Soul and lose a little more stability.

These identifications are very unstable, as they are based on disharmony, so they need to feed regularly. They buzz around in the mind constantly, seeking to agitate and catch our attention to inspire thinking. The thought "I am ugly" now leads us into thinking about being ugly, for example, by way of remembering a time when we were told we were ugly and how that made us feel, or maybe by going into a problem-solving mode to consider how we might be less ugly through applying makeup or getting our hair done, etc.

Many teachings say that we should make positive statements to ourselves such as, "I am confident," but those statements create and sustain identifications just as surely as do negative statements. Consider any activity that you are truly confident at, and pay attention to the mind when doing it. If there is true confidence, there is total silence in relation to that activity.

Speculation, concepts, theories, and belief systems all come about as a result of ignorance and a sense of otherness. However, present moment curiosity and questioning do not bind Soul, because they are open. What binds energy is thinking, speculation, and the conclusions that we create to answer our own questions because all thinking, speculation, and conclusions come from our pre-existing paradigm, our perspective on the world, which means thinking, speculation, and conclusions all come from the past. Another common form of binding happens when we blindly accept the conclusions of others without having any insight. To blindly believe anything without insight, whether true or false, is to bind Soul energy.

Businesses, cultures, societies are all built around thoughts, concepts, theories, and beliefs. And all are of the mind, which means they feed identifications. Thus, identifications do not affect just the individual; they spread their seed and affect communities. When enough people accept a concept, theory, or belief, then external structures, cultures, and traditions are built around the accepted concept, theory, or belief. Once a concept or belief reaches the stage of popularity, tradition, or "fact," it's very tough for the individual to speak or act against the tradition or "fact" due to the backlash of the majority. How can the individual be honest about something when one's reputation, income, business, lifestyle, social position, sense of self, and so forth rest on a commonly accepted falsehood? Can we stare in the face of the accepted falsehood and tell the truth when it may cost us our position, our marriage, our status, our friends? Building communities around falsehoods that will cause endless frustration and disharmony to maintain – it's an identification's dream.

The more powerful identifications, especially ones related to trauma, will try to convince us that we need them to survive; that they help us or protect us. Justification and pride are perfect examples, as they tend to work together in convincing us that, no matter our wrongs, we must defend our words and actions and never admit our mistakes. Of course, this causes tremendous disharmony, but pride and justification tell us otherwise, or blame will accuse someone else.

Shame is another identification, one that tries to get us to admit our wrongs by beating us down emotionally. "You should be ashamed of yourself" and "I am ashamed of myself" are perfect examples of shame's negative influence. Of course, admitting a mistake is extremely important, but we should admit the mistake out of rightness, not shame.

A perfect example of shame is a story a single mother once told me. When her only son was about eight years old, he and his friends stole a hood ornament off a Mercedes-Benz. A mother of one of his friends found the ornament and realized her son had stolen it. She called the school to report the crime. All the parents involved were summoned to the school to meet with the principal and were shocked that their kids had stolen.

When the mother, who told me this story, returned home with her son, she took him to his bedroom and asked him, "Why did you do something like that? It's wrong to steal." If she had stopped there she would not have fed or created shame, but she continued: "You know you are my only son, and you don't have a father. If you do something good, people will think, 'Wow, he was raised in a good way, even without a father. His mom must be great. But if you do bad things like this, people will think negatively of kids raised by single mothers.'"

Even though this story occurred many decades ago, the mother regrets evoking shame because she feels that, after that talk, her son began repressing himself. Many times parents use emotion such as crying to try to amplify the feeling of shame. This only feeds identifications further. Of course, the child may stop wrong behavior because of shame, but it conditions the parent and the child in unhealthy ways and exacts a toll on Soul.

Identifications like this can entrap entire societies. We can see this phenomenon at the national level, where no matter the destructive actions of one nation against another nation, many in the perpetrating society get angry if the leader apologizes for the destructive action, feeling that to apologize is to admit weakness. But just as we do not respect a person who justifies and is too prideful to admit mistakes, neither does the world respect a country that refuses to apologize. The true damage is not in the arena of public opinion, though, but at the level of Soul. If we justify or defend our mistakes, we are destined to repeat them, and each time we do, a sliver of Soul is served up.

The best way to stop feeding these types of identifications is to admit mistakes up front, even if no one confronted us on those mistakes. An ex-convict friend of mine, Steve, long ago exemplified this principle to me. He had told a self-inflating lie in our conversation, which I failed to notice, but to my surprise, he said, "I don't know what came over me, but what I said isn't true." He then explained the actuality. I was stunned because I had never witnessed this type of honesty before in my life. The respect I had for him at that moment was beyond measure.

Steve's honesty so surprised me that my curiosity redirected the conversation into how he came by this method of honesty. He told me that during his stay in prison, his roommate, Lauren, was an older man and a very sincere, repentant Christian. When they were out on the yard, Steve had gotten into a verbal confrontation with another inmate. Steve was clearly in the wrong, but he would never admit it. When he and Lauren got back to their cell, Lauren said, "I have noticed for a long time that you have difficulty admitting when you are wrong. It's hard to admit you are wrong, but you need to do it once, which will be really hard, but after that it gets easy. Then it doesn't really matter if you are wrong, because you don't get mad anymore. Instead, you will be able to laugh about it, and you will be a much better person. You just say, 'Ah, I see. You are right.' Lauren continued, 'You don't even have to say that you are wrong; just agree with the other person if they are right.'" My friend started to apply this honesty deeply in his life. I so loved the feeling of this that it planted a seed in me to be honest like that whenever my mouth rode a lie.

It's not weakness to admit a mistake, but strength, if the admission was done out of rightness, not shame. That being said, there may be people who will try to take advantage of our admission, in an attempt to shame us. Be aware that it's not them abusing us, but their identifications speaking through them, trying to feed. Of course, the person will not realize this, and it will only make things worse at that moment to teach them. If we get upset by the criticism, then we are just feeding more identifications. It's healthy to sincerely apologize without expecting it to be accepted. If the apology is not accepted, we allow for that while correcting ourselves. We do not make the other person our project.

When we understand how energy is bound in identifications and how to unbind that energy, we begin opening up to answers through insight and not through thinking, which is of the mind. In this way, we are able to understand things directly. This occurs naturally in the latter stages of unfoldment as the mind begins to quiet more and more. And this insight further expedites our unfoldment if we make use of it.

One of the functions of emotion is to reflect thought as it comes through the body, but emotion is not limited to being direct expressions of such thought. While thought-identifications are created from identifying the self with such statements as "I am smart," emotion-identifications(8) are born in a more subtle way through simple association. We may never have had the structured thought "I am angry," for example, but still can have energy bound up in anger. Although emotion does function in part as a physical representation of thought, there is more to emotion than just being a reflection of thought. The mind is like a deep ocean that has many layers. There are the obvious layers of thought and emotion that are like the waves at the surface. But below the surface are many layers and currents that are less obvious. These layers are what I call meaning associations. Which is to say, we have impregnated experiences and words with certain associations.

A perfect example of these hidden associations is an experience that two of my mentoring students had by the campfire one night. I had built a good fire before they arrived, then I had them get into a good meditation and marked their energy field edge. Both students

were quite expanded. Finally I led them to the campfire. As soon as
they came near the fire both of their energy fields shrank down and
they were back into mind. I pointed this out to them and asked them
if they knew why they had collapsed back into mind. They both
thought about it for a moment, and then one responded, "I don't
know; I like campfires, so I would have thought that my energy field
would have expanded as I neared this fire."

I said, "Well, energy fields do not lie. You believe you like
campfires, and that appears to be true if we look only at the surface
of your mind, but deeper down there is a negative meaning
associated with fire that you are not aware of right now." They
meditated on these words and searched their bodies when they
neared the fire. They found that, indeed, there was a subtle feeling in
the body that arose whenever they got to a certain distance from the
fire, and at that very moment their energy fields began to shrink
dramatically. As it turned out, both of them had suffered traumatic
burns as young children. They had all but forgotten the injuries, but
the association had taken root. In the deeper recesses of the mind,
that association was still alive and influencing their experience. That
was an emotion-identification born of an unresolved painful
experience. Both of these students resolved that identification, and
their energy fields no longer collapsed when they neared the fire.

Interestingly, before they had resolved the fire association, we did
a little experiment with words. Even saying the word *fire* would
cause them to collapse back into mind. Later we experimented with
other words and their effect on the tuning process. What we found
was that many of the words that they thought they had purely
positive associations with were actually causing collapse. Many of the
"positive" words that we hold dear, like *love, honor, courage,
respect,* and so on are heavily tainted with disharmony in the deeper
recesses of mind. In fact, for the vast majority of individuals, their
entire vocabulary is heavily tainted, which means that language itself
becomes a huge hurdle, blocking us from tuning to consciousness.

With regard to an emotional identification with anger, the
association often occurs during events where we felt that anger made
us powerful. Once there is an association between anger and power,
every time anger arises, we unconsciously flame it with Soul energy
because we like feeling powerful. Anger then becomes a primary
emotional strategy.

The base levels feelings are vulnerability, fear, aloneness, and a bracing against change. The most basic emotions are agitation and frustration, so we want to be very aware of these energies within the body. For most identifications, the most lucrative way to harvest food is to make an individual so uncomfortable that the individual starts trying to escape the present moment by projecting into the future or the past through imagination and thinking, which is psychological time. As the individual reacts to agitation, Soul energy is siphoned off by the identification, which when full goes into a state of torpor and ceases to agitate for a time.

Emotional tendencies come from associating emotion with the self. A person may have unconsciously associated himself or herself with being a kind person. In such a case, that individual has actually created an emotion-identification called kindness, which produces a weak energy projection around the body attracting those who would wish to take advantage of that weakness. Kindness then uses our bodies like puppets to express itself and cause disharmony. How is that bad? Kindness makes it difficult for the individual to say, "No" when "No" is the most appropriate answer. This then causes a tremendous amount of stress on the individual, which feeds the identification. When resolved to Soul there is naturally love, gentleness, and service, but there is also the capacity to draw a line when one needs to be drawn because the energy is stable.

All of the traumas of our lives are emotion-identifications. The bigger the trauma, the more powerful the identification. These identifications create such strong emotional urges when they rise up, out of torpor, that resisting them may be nearly impossible. An extreme example of this sort of trauma identification is when a young child has been sexually molested. Oftentimes when the child matures they gain a very unhealthy sexual expression that may result in wanting to be sexually dominated or the opposite. Many individuals who were sexually abused as children may not even remember it because the trauma was so overwhelming that it was blocked out of accessible memory. Even if they can't recall the abuse, they still carry the trauma that acts out through unhealthy sexuality.

Weaker identifications may come out in common relationship arguments amplifying distrust, judgmentalism, and aggression. Here is a common example I hear regularly: "I know that making that negative comment to my partner is not going to help, but I say it anyway, and we end up in an argument. The funny thing is, I am aware enough to know that I shouldn't say it, but often enough I end up saying it anyway. And when I say it, it even kind of feels good — like I scored a point or won. Of course, my partner gets really upset, and we end up in a terrible argument." This situation perfectly exemplifies what I mean when I say the individual was unconscious. They were not actually in control of themselves; they were in the passenger's seat. Their control was usurped by emotion-identifications well before they actually said that hurtful thing. Signs of an identification coming out of torpor need to be noticed at a very early stage, before the identification fully awakens. Otherwise, it's often too late and the odds of successfully piloting harmoniously through the situation are greatly diminished.

It may have been just one identification or several that urged the individual to say something hurtful, but regardless of how many created the urge, certainly many identifications fed off of both individuals during the argument. Identifications are not concerned with marital happiness; they are concerned only with feeding and will do whatever it takes to get us to act or react in negative ways.

Even though it was an identification that spoke those hurtful words, we cannot say, "The Devil made me do it," can we? Yes, it was an identification that took over and controlled the body like a puppet, but the individual is solely responsible for it. We are responsible for all that expresses through the body, either consciously or unconsciously. Imagine this scenario: A police officer is using a bullhorn in hopes of bringing a crowd under control. Someone comes up to the officer and asks to use the bullhorn, and the officer agrees. That person uses the bullhorn to enflame the crowd, and violence results. Doesn't the officer bear responsibility for lending the bullhorn to someone else to use? Absolutely. Similarly, we bear responsibility for all that we allow to express through our bodies, for we have empowered all of it, even if unwittingly.

With regard to deeply traumatic identifications, they can cause a person to jump into a fight, flight, avoidance state, heart-rate elevated, blood pressure up, and bladder constricted, just as if in actual physical danger. A person in this state is highly unstable, and even the most innocuous, well-meaning comment could easily be misconstrued as a personal attack. The body always mirrors the type of energy that is within the mind, so if we are observing the body, we can become aware of what was formerly unconscious. A common sign that strong identifications are taking over is a feeling of detached emptiness that will enable a person to be unfeelingly cruel and harsh. Ideally we will notice a subtle feeling of agitation, tension, or even dullness in the body. It's often most obvious in the chest because our breathing is altered. As you become more aware, you will be able to feel how different frequencies of disharmony tend to show up in different parts of the body. By observing this, we can become tremendously aware of other individual's disharmony as those frequencies also reflect in our own bodies in subtle ways.

I have seen longtime friendships ended over deep-seated traumas arising unexpectedly. One individual felt belittled and never spoke to her best friend again. Sadly, her friend and all witnesses had absolutely no idea what had happened to cause the relationship to end. It was an unsalvageable mess.

We also steal attention, and it causes tremendous disharmony. Have you ever felt how draining it is to be in the vicinity of certain individuals? Probably everyone knows individuals who are constantly seeking either "positive" attention by showing off or seeking compliments or "negative" attention by way of sympathy. Really, it does not matter whether the attention is positive or negative, so a person may do all they can just to get us angry. All they are seeking is the reactive attention that we give them. Some individuals have gotten so stuck in the rut of attention-vampirism that they annoy everyone around them without even trying.

A less obvious way is through success and performance. Many athletes and entertainers, for example, egoicly feed off of the attention they receive. They are vampiring. What is happening here is the identification in another person is siphoning off the energy of those people around them through emotional attention. The attention, no matter the form, is not beneficial to the receiver, as it is not love.

Let's look at an example of an adult who is actively participating in energy vampirism: the gossip. This person spends every available moment getting people's attention in order to gossip about other people. The gossip gains an initial emotional high from the attention given them through the gossip process, right? But because energy received is absorbed by identifications, the high that the person feels is the frenzy of the feast. Then, of course, other identifications feed on the chaos created from the aftereffects of gossip: lack of trust, frustration, victimization, etc. Truly, a whole host is fed, but the humans involved only lose energy. People participating in negativity actually gain nothing of true value from it. They merely provide for an identification banquet, further degrade themselves, and pull other people down with them. That is, of course, until they have insight into this process, and then, little by little, they cease investing in insanity.

Sensing, emotion, thought, imagination, and memory work synergistically to make up the matrix of the mind, which keeps one from being present. Whenever we go into judgment or comparisons with regard to the self or others; whenever we fail to forgive ourselves or others; whenever we get nostalgic for the past or look forward to the future, we are stepping out of the present. Each time we allow the mind to leap forward or backward in time for emotional reasons, it binds Soul into darkness. The darkness takes on an identity of its own and now needs us to feed it. Each time we slip into distraction, willfulness, or brace against the moment, we feed something. Anytime we aren't fully present and tuned to unconditioned love, something is siphoning off our energy.

Nothing can steal our energy unless we wrongly give of it through an inappropriate response. So, it's useless to go into blame, which is yet another identification. The way to properly manage one's energy is to remain present, calm, and tuned to the frequencies of consciousness, while taking total authority over and responsibility for one's energy. The solution begins right now, within each of us, by tuning to an unconditionally loving, stable, and peaceful state as often as possible. When we collapse out of consciousness and into the mind, we take notice and open back up again. The more we do this, the freer we all are.

~Chapter 21~
Unconditioned Love

> The spirit of Buddha is that of great loving-kindness and
> compassion.
>
> — *The Teachings of Buddha*

We can see that unconditioned love has been recognized as the spiritual alchemical agent for many thousands of years, because the teachings of Christianity, Buddhism, and most other major religions indicate it as the great vehicle of transformation. Given love's prominent position among religions, why hasn't the world already been transformed by this alchemy?

Is the violent and forceful state of the world a failure of love? If unconditioned love truly is the alchemical agent of transformation, which is being taught to the estimated 500 million Buddhists and 2 billion Christians, roughly a third of the 7 billion humans on the planet, then why is it that the earth is so fraught with disharmony, war, and division? Could it be that unconditioned love is not what is being taught?

Looking into it, Soul cannot be taught because it's the default and merely needs to be revealed in order to be active in one's life. Even if the teacher is resolved to Soul and therefore unconditioned love, if the listener is tuned to mind, any teachings are quite naturally filtered through the mind, which brings the teachings into a frequency of disharmony regardless of the words used in the teaching. Thanks to the filters of the mind, the love that people are learning through religion is idealized(9), which is to say it's in the frequency of ideas or concepts, and, therefore, it is thought(9), which also represents in the body as emotion(8). There is no transformative power in thought or emotion. So, even though the teacher uses the words *unconditioned love*, unconditioned love(13+) is not actualized by the listener.

Could not an evil-minded person hide behind the words

unconditioned love? Any person, regardless of moral or ethical standing, can use words like *love* to mislead people, which proves that the words *unconditioned love* do not have transformative power. If those words had transformative power, then any evil-minded individual would fear to use them because it would undermine their identification with evil. Words are of thought and are therefore not transformative. We need to go beyond words in order to find harmony.

Apart from the idea(9) of love, there is another expression of love that we will address here for edification purposes: personal love(8). Personal love is what we feel for our family, our friends, our pets, etc. The intensity of personal love will naturally vary, depending upon the specific relationship. A nurturing mother's feeling of love for her baby may far exceed the intensity of the love she feels for a friend. Regardless of the object of the love, it's still personal and not unconditioned love. Someone may believe that they love their child unconditionally, but there is still a condition in that the love is exclusive to the child, which means it's not truly unconditioned.

Emotional vulnerability and affection are often confused with unconditioned love, but both affection and emotional vulnerability are frequencies of the mind and are quite distinct from the frequencies of unconditioned love. Emotional vulnerability is something to be shared only with the most trusted individuals in our personal lives. To share this energy openly with just anyone is likely to open us up to a lot of abuse. Affection is an energy that will reward any state of mind, even a destructive state. If expressed at the wrong time, affection will exacerbate unstable behavior. And since no life-form can be happy when emotionally unstable, to give affection at the wrong time causes psychological harm.

Because emotional vulnerability opens one to abuse and because affection rewards even destructive behavior, both of these energies need to be expressed very judiciously, so as not to cause harm. Unconditioned love, though, has no vulnerabilities; it defuses disharmonious intention and behavior, and, therefore, it's always appropriate.

Within the frequencies of emotion there is a large variety encompassing both positive and negative energies. Within personal love we have those frequencies that are for our pets, our children, our friends, our parents. Some of these relationships will resonate at much higher frequencies than others. This is normal and natural.

Just as there is a gradation in the frequencies of personal love, there is also a frequency gradation covering types of anger. There is frustration, anger, rage, hatred, and a whole host of other emotions between each of these levels of hostility for which there aren't even words. In the emotional spectrum, there is a large frequency range encompassing a tremendous breadth of emotional possibilities, many of which are so subtly different that there are no words to describe them.

If we were to divide the frequencies of emotion in half, the lower half of the emotional spectrum would be purely disharmonious, meaning that tuning to these frequencies is detrimental to the body and has no direct benefit. Such emotions would be feelings of victimization, uselessness, purposelessness, jealousy, anger, blame, negative expectation, doubt, boredom, etc. The upper half of the frequencies have beneficial aspects to go with their inherent disharmonious aspects. Examples of these double-edged emotions are positive expectation, hopefulness, optimism, faith, enthusiasm, passion, love, etc.

"Positive" emotions are always tethered to "negative" emotions, so whatever goes up must come down. We have hope(8), but then the hope is dashed by an unwanted outcome. We then feel hopeless. Looking at hope even further, is not hope born of negativity? We are unhappy or dissatisfied with the present, so we hope for a better future. Hope, as it comes from the mind, is always for the future, which means it's an escape from the present. It's a judgment against the present situation of our life, is it not?

I am not saying that these energies are not important. Everything serves a purpose, and we need emotion until we no longer need it. We need thought until we no longer need it. Emotion and thought are not wrong, nor are they right; they simply are. For this reason, we cannot force ourselves or someone else into unfoldment. Once we have matured and are ready to begin consciously unfolding, we can make productive use of our intention through meditation and daily living toward global awareness and unconditioned love. But even when we are ready to begin the unfoldment process, it will take time because there is a lot of bound energy to resolve; also because the body needs to adjust to the changes over time. Just as there is no benefit to being impatient with the body's maturation process, there is no benefit to impatience with the process of unfoldment.

This brings us to the conscious frequency of unconditioned love.

No one can teach what unconditioned love is because it's not of the mind. Unconditioned love can only be inspirienced. We cannot create it because it's innately present yet typically inactive. What we can do is tune to it and activate it, which will bring us into the frequency of unconditioned love(13+), the great alchemical agent that purifies and unveils.

Consider this African proverb: "When there is no enemy within, the enemies outside cannot hurt you." An individual who is stabilized in unconditioned love sufficiently has a field of protection around them that wards off malicious intent. The effect is such that the would-be attacker's body refuses to launch the attack, feeling fear as their own dark intent is mirrored back at them. This is the natural effect of unconditioned love. This protection remains so long as the individual is centered in unconditioned love. If this stable individual were to go into emotional vulnerability or affection, he or she would be vulnerable. For this reason, if we are going to actualize unconditioned love in our lives, we must clearly realize the difference between consciousness and mind; otherwise we will habitually be tuning to mind and, therefore, suffering.

~Chapter 22~
The Bones of Christ

There is no fear in love; but perfect love casts out fear,
because fear involves torment.
But he who fears has not been made perfect in love.

— 1 John, The New Testament

For many thousands of years, much of humankind has followed the code of Hammurabi and the law of Moses, which are based on "an eye for an eye, a tooth for a tooth." The idea is that justice is made through equal and opposite vengeance. This mentality often leads to the escalation of violence. We can see by the state of the world that violence, revenge, and punishment are not transformative energies.

Several thousand years ago a distinctly new option was introduced to the world through the teachings of both Siddhartha Gautama and Jesus of Nazareth. Through Jesus' story we call it the way of the cross. Siddhartha described it as the way of suffering. This path is exemplified by Jesus' admonition as recorded in Matthew 5:39, "But I tell you not to resist an evil person. But whoever slaps you on your right cheek, turn the other to him also."

Nearly a century ago Mohandas Gandhi, in a testimonial to the idea of such nonviolence, insightfully asserted, "An eye for an eye will leave everyone blind." Through nonviolence Gandhi led India to independence from Great Britain, which had enslaved that country under a then-legal but immoral construct wherein white people dominated people of color.

Although Gandhi's use of nonviolent resistance led to the liberation of India from British rule, the world has not fully embraced this courageous, love-based approach, and nearly a century later we are still stuck in revenge and punishment. Fundamentally, when push comes to shove, people believe that violence is more effective than love, and, as a result, all of the structures of humankind are based on force and violence in the final analysis. How does Turn the Other Cheek work? It's a nonviolent way of resisting oppression and violence while maintaining the dignity of superior moral position. When you are attacked, you calmly accept the attack while maintaining the moral high ground. By this means the oppressor's very attack is proof that they do not have a moral foothold, which lowers their standing in the public eye. Moreover, a person with any shred of conscience will not be able to maintain hostility as he begins to feel the dignity and humanity of the oppressed.

Nonviolence has proved to be an incredibly powerful way of dealing with the aggression and corruption of the world. Through this strategy, Martin Luther King and others in the Civil Rights marches of the 1960s made huge progress against the U.S. government and the dominant white society in desegregating the United States and improving the social status of women and minority peoples around the world.

Nonviolent resistance has proved to be extremely powerful, but it's not a bulletproof strategy. Because it's a strategy that has conditions which it depends upon to be successful, it can be countered. The conditions required for nonviolent resistance to be successful are a just cause, a clear message, dignity, and the moral high ground. The counter to nonviolent resistance is to create the appearance that one or more of these conditions is lacking. If, for example, the oppressor can stimulate the protesters to become violent, to lose dignity or the moral high ground, or, at least, create the image that the protesters are violent, undignified, or immoral by infiltrating their ranks, then the protest will not be respected by the larger community and it will fail. We saw this occur during the Occupy Movement, and it's now a common strategy to tarnish the image of protesters around the world.

Nonviolence is a high ideal that was transmitted to the world through individuals such as Jesus and Siddhartha for the purpose of bringing us up to a higher law, which is unconditioned love. The time to actualize this higher law is now. Imagine a protest that is so lovingly nonviolent and dignified that authorities and infiltrators alike are rendered unable to attack, their malicious intent preventing them from being able to swing their batons, spray their mace, or vandalize property. Imagine the seed of consciousness planted in the hearts of the aggressors as they realize that violence, force, and fear have no power over unconditioned love.

The more people tune to unconditioned love, the easier it is for subsequent people to do so, and the more profound the effects. I see that the practice of tuning to unconditioned love will spread among the populaces of the world, ending anger, violence, and aggression of all sorts. Imagine a nation practicing unconditioned love so thoroughly that terrorism is rendered entirely ineffective as fear turns to love. Would there be any need of a military? Would we need police? When people understand that unconditioned love trumps all other strategies, what would the world look like? We are on the cusp of the greatest revelation in human history, which is actually a revolution. It's a revolution of the heart that will affect all of the structures of humanity for the benefit of all life.

As a young boy I awoke to find Jesus Christ lying on the floor, his eyes filled with sorrow, his body lacking bones. "Find my bones, for they are the core of my teaching. Find the essence of my teaching and give it back to the world," he requested. I have spent more than 30 years looking for those bones. I have crisscrossed the globe multiple times in the search. I have read and contemplated. I have meditated and prayed, and through all of it, I was like a blind man fumbling around in a briar maze, not knowing where the exit was. Again and again I crashed face-first into the walls, my flesh torn away. But against all logic, there was something goading me on. "There has to be a way out," I thought. After years of bumps and bruises, scratches and tears, I have finally realized there is no way out. But there is a way in.

For more than three decades I have trained and dedicated myself to martial, healing, and spiritual paths, having achieved the highest rankings and titles. But at the very core, unrealized even by many individuals teaching these arts, there is the same fundamental thing, the marrow if you will. Each person that I have met, whether "civilized" or "primitive," male or female, old or young, has at their very core this very same marrow, which is Soul.

What are the essential teachings of Jesus, the bones of Christ? Without hesitation, I declare unconditioned love to be the bones of Christ. Without hesitation, I declare unconditioned love to be the bones of Buddha. Without hesitation, I declare unconditioned love to be the essence of any true teaching. This is the essential teaching of all Graduated Souls, the true masters. This is the ultimate path for all individuals regardless of ancestry, culture, deeds, or name. It's only through unconditioned love that anyone realizes true mastery.

The vision in the Amazon said, "There is conscious light from the center of the galaxy, bathing the earth with ever-increasing intensity." I now see that we will meet that light with the conscious light of our being, bathing the entire multiverse in unconditioned love and thereby resolving all sense of separation. In this way, there may be no need for the collapse of humankind and the probable futures of Hell on Earth. Instead, we will transition into an environmentally sustainable, spiritually fulfilling, socially just human presence on this planet.

All that is, is within you, and you are within it; there is no other. There is absolutely no judgment or negativity of any sort. There is perfect forgiveness, for there is unconditioned love. Although there is the ability to perceive the illusion of negativity, there is no binding, fear, or ignorance, only total harmony and understanding.

"So be perfect, as your heavenly Father is perfect." This is not only a possibility for all; it's inevitable. There is a presence, intelligence, and power so perfect, so loving that no human words can adequately describe it, and it's you. Now is the time to awaken from the dream of otherness to the realization of unconditioned love. There is no other. Now is the time to prove it to yourself and the world. Are you ready?

Many Blessings,

Richard L. Haight
www.richardhaight.net

If you'd like to support the message of this work, there are many ways to do so. Writing a review, tweeting, or sharing is very helpful. You could gift a copy to a friend in need. Another great way to help is to ask your favorite book store to carry *The Unbound Soul*.

Acknowledgments

In Memory of Ethan McMillan (Feb 18, 2005 - Feb 22, 2016)

First, my humble and heartfelt appreciation goes to my martial arts instructor Shizen Osaki, who set aside a tremendous amount of time to help me explore this path of spiritual unfoldment. You have been more than a teacher to me; you have been a partner in this process and a dear friend. Bless you and thank you, Sensei.

To my students, I offer my thanks for your curiosity and dedication to the unfoldment process.

I'd like to thank Reverend Jean Holms and Coy Johnston for their support at a very delicate time in my life and for continually encouraging me to write my experiences and insights.

To Steve Wieck, thank you for graciously lending your expertise with regard to the maze that is the book publishing process., and ultimately introducing me to my copy editor, Ed Hall of Hallworks Productions.

To Ed Hall of Hallworks Productions, I extend my deepest appreciation for the transformative work you did on the manuscript. Your insight and integrity beam through the copy editing such that upon reading the corrected manuscript I was moved to tears.

To Hester Lee Furey, my proof reader, who lovingly polished the text into its final luster, you have my deepest gratitude.

To Justin Hager and to my father, Gordon Haight, I thank you for the feedback on the early drafts of this work which greatly served to streamline the book.

To my wife, Teruko: thank you for your undying support and patience through the writing of this book and for being my life partner. Words fail me.

Contributors

Self-publishing is an expensive enterprise, and I have been blessed with the support of many generous individuals whose financial contributions have allowed for publishing.

1. Masaya Higuma
2. Gordon Haight
3. Kris Kokay
4. Shizen Osaki
5. Kathryn Reppond
6. Fuyuo Sato
7. Eri Sato
8. Kaoru Ohara
9. Celina Reppond
10. Kuriko Kanke
11. Nobutaka Aoki
12. Hitomi Aoki
13. Kotomi Aoki
14. Kotetsu Aoki
15. Diane Ferdig
16. Neal Ferdig
17. Naoki Takakuwa
18. Hitomi Chishima
19. Camille Arredondo
20. Steve Haight
21. Coy Johnston

Glossary

Emotion a strong feeling (such as love, anger, joy, hate, or fear); feelings.

Expectation a belief that something will happen or is likely to happen.

Feeling the undifferentiated background of one's awareness considered apart from any identifiable sensation, perception, or thought.

Feeling Associations a taint associated with experiences and words which has been unconsciously impregnated into the sense of self at a very fundamental level; Meaning Associations.

Feelings emotional states or reactions.

Identification a largely unconscious process whereby an individual models thoughts, feelings, and actions after those attributed to an object that has been incorporated as a mental image.

Ignorance described in this work as willfully focusing to exclusion in order to come to a conclusion.

Imagination the ability to imagine things that are not real: the ability to form a picture in your mind of something that you have not seen or experienced.

Innocence freedom from guilt or sin through being unacquainted with evil.

Insight a direct understanding of the true nature of something.

Inspirience any unconditioned experience; its roots are inspire and experience.

Isness the most fundamental foundation of all that is. Formless yet throughout all form. Soul and Isness are interchangeable terms indicating the same thing.

Meaning Association a taint associated with experiences and words which has been unconsciously impregnated into the sense of self at a very fundamental level; Feeling Associations.

Memory the power or process of remembering what has been learned.

Persona a mask that the individual has created over many lifetimes to protect the self and/or to gain a social advantage. Interchangeable with *personality* in this work.

Self Content the accumulated meaning associations, feelings/emotions, memories, and thoughts which have become the definition and sense of who and what one is and which are the ultimate source of suffering; identifications.

Senses the five natural powers (touch, taste, smell, sight, and hearing) through which you receive information about the world around you.

Soul the most fundamental foundation of all that is. Formless yet throughout all form. Soul and Isness are interchangeable terms indicating the same thing.

Spirit the non-physical self-image-template of the individual life-form within the multiverse.

Thought an idea, plan, opinion, picture, etc., that is formed in your mind: something that you think of.

Appendix

Electromagnetic Spectrum Classes:
1 - Radio
2 - Microwave
3 - Infrared
4 - Visible
5 - Ultraviolet
6 - X-ray
7 - Gamma ray

Mental Spectrum Classes:
8 - Emotion, Feelings, Will
9 - Thought, Imagination, Memory

Harmonious Frequency Classes:
10 - Curiosity, Relaxation, Innocence
11 - Observation, Sharing, Compassion
12 - Silence, Acceptance, Appreciation
13+ - Unconditioned Love

Notes

Biblical Scripture taken from the New King James Version®. Copyright © 1982 by Thomas Nelson. Used by permission. All rights reserved.

Quotes taken from Tao Te Ching by Stephen Mitchell. © 2016 Stephen Mitchell. Published by HARPERCOLLINS 1988.

Quotes taken from THE TEACHINGS OF BUDDHA. Copyright © 1966 BUKKYO DENDO KYOKAI (One hundred & sixtieth revised edition, 1989).

Inspirience
Meditation Unbound
The Unconditioned Path to Spiritual Awakening

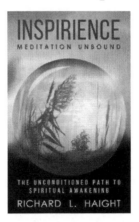

EXPERIENCING LIFE
INSPIRING CHANGE
LIVING INSPIRIENCE

What is it you truly seek? The reality is, most of us don't really know. Upon close investigation, we discover, above all else, we are seeking the transcendent, that which resides at the deepest place within us, that which connects us to all that *is* and gives unconditioned meaning to our lives.

The transcendent exceeds the grasp of the mind and the limits of words, for it is beyond all form and definition. But inspirience, although it cannot be explained in words, can be found. There is a path to it.

Richard L. Haight, bestselling author of *The Unbound Soul*, shares a simple and natural way to inspirience through unconditioned meditation. *Inspirience* will take you on a journey to the transcendent, *so that it can transform your life—and the world.*

Have you wanted to incorporate meditation into your life, but find it almost impossible to start? Inspirience will open the doors wide to you.

- Learn how to actively apply meditation to your daily life, not just your living room. Once you try this approach, you won't go back.

- Learn what is truly blocking your inner peace, purpose, and productivity - this fundamental imbalance has been overlooked in spiritual teachings for thousands of years.

- Learn how to bring true purpose and meaning into your life and thereby transcend the lurking feelings of frustration, emptiness, and loneliness.

- Learn how to root the mind in consciousness, so that you gain the productivity that the mind can provide, along with the peace that comes with consciousness.

- Discover the nature of conscience and the incredible power hidden there just waiting to be tapped.

"I read one spiritual book a week for my radio show, and I will tell you that Inspirience is fresh, genuine, and much needed"
—Jean Adrienne, PowerTalk Radio

"I had the privilege of reading Richard's book before it was published; I am still amazed by it even now!"
— Billy Atwell, FEAR NOT podcast

"Extremely valuable, challenging and wisdom-full - it could be a real gift and catalyst for a spiritual exploration and healing."
—Jane Derry, Serenity Vista Treatment for Alcoholism

Dance of the Self
Moving Beyond Suffering

Coming early 2018

For more information visit www.richardhaight.net

Made in the USA
Middletown, DE
02 November 2017